Dearest
Enjoy
the anti
Chinese paintings & words
With much love,
fleur

Selections from the Book of Poetry

(Illustrated Edition)

精选诗经与诗意画

（英汉对照）

CHINA INTERCONTINENTAL PRESS
五洲传播出版社

Contents

目 录

秦风

陈风

桧风

曹风

豳风

小　雅

鹿鸣之什

南有嘉鱼之什

鸿雁之什

节南山之什

甫田之什

鱼藻之什

大　雅

文王之什

生民之什

颂

商　颂

Preface

Liu Fengwen

The Book of Poetry, China's first ancient poem collection, was compiled in the middle of the Spring and Autumn Period, around the 6th century BC, and roughly contemporary with the epics *Iliad* and *Odyssey* by Homer of ancient Greece. At the beginning it was called *Poetry*, *300 Poems* or *Collected 300 Poems*. It didn't have its current name until the Western Han Dynasty (206 BC-AD 25) when it was regarded as a Confucian classic and listed in the "Six Classics" along with *Collection of Ancient Texts*, *The Rites*, *The Book of Music*, *The Book of Changes* and *The Spring and Autumn Annals*.

Its compiler has been usually ascribed to Confucius, ancient Chinese educator. According to *Historical Records* by Sima Qian, historian of the Western Han Dynasty, prior to Confucius' time, there were over 3,000 poems in circulation. After strict screening, Confucius saved only 305 and used them and the other five classics as textbooks to teach his disciples.

During the Han Dynasty annotating and teaching *The Book of Poetry* were four schools, founded respectively by Yuan Gu of the Qi State, Shen Pei of the Lu State, Han Ying of the Yan State, Mao Heng of the Lu State and Mao Chang of the Zhao State. Nonetheless, only the edition annotated by Mao Heng and Mao Chang was handed down to this very day.

Poems included in *The Book of Poetry* were written approximately between the early years of the Western Zhou Dynasty (11th century BC) and the middle of the Spring and Autumn Period (6th century BC), dating back about 2,500 years.

Legend goes that official collectors went on a special mission to solicit folk songs and ballads from Gansu, Shaanxi, Shanxi, Hebei, Henan, Shandong and Hubei, and presented them to the imperial court of the Zhou Dynasty. Some other poems in the book are odes to the Zhou king, composed by high court officials and the literati. Imperial musicians then wrote music for all the poems to amuse the king.

The Book of Poetry divides into three parts: the Book of Songs, the Book of Odes and Epics, and the Book of Hymns, consisting of 305 poems.

Contained in the Book of Songs are poems collected south of the Zhou capital (modern Shaanxi and Henan) and around the capital (modern Henan), south of Shao (modern Henan), in Bei (modern Hebei), Yong (modern Shandong), Wei (modern Henan), Zheng (modern Henan),

Qi (modern Shandong), Wei (modern Shanxi), Tang (modern Shanxi), Qin (modern Shaanxi), Chen (modern Henan), Gui (modern Henan), Cao (modern Shandong) and Bin (modern Shaanxi). This volume includes a total of 160 poems, most of which are folk songs circulated and sung in the Yellow, Yangtze and Hanshui river valleys.

Of the 105 poems in the Book of Odes and Epics, a majority were written by the nobles and sung in the imperial court; only a small part in the Book of Odes were created by folk poets. The Book of Hymns, including hymns of Zhou, Lu and Shang, consists of 40 sacrificial songs.

The Book of Poetry is composed mainly of lyrics, coupled with narrative poems, satirical poems and ballads. It gives a vivid description of various aspects of social life during the Zhou Dynasty, mirrors the sufferings of the people brought about by war and heavy corvée, and extols their pursuing love and freedom. Therefore, the book is both a literary treasure and important data for socio-historical study of ancient China.

Three rhetorical methods -- *fu* (narration), *bi* (simile) and *xing* (borrowed analogy) -- have been used in *The Book of Poetry* to enhance its power of expression. With high artistic attainments, it has been an imperishable literary masterpiece both in China and the world, and a dazzling pearl in the long river of human history, producing a far-reaching impact on literary creation of later ages.

In history it had become a tradition to illustrate *The Book of Poetry* with pictures or produce works of art themed on its poems owing to the book's charm and reputation. Of those being handed down, the *Illustration of The Book of Poetry* transcribed by Emperor Gaozong of the Southern Song Dynasty and illustrated by noted painter Ma Hezhi is perhaps the most widespread one. Its editions have been kept respectively in the Palace Museum of Beijing, Shanghai Municipal Museum, Liaoning Provincial Museum, Palace Museum of Taipei, Museum of Guangxi Zhuang Autonomous Region, Museum of Fine Arts in Boston, Metropolitan Museum of Art in New York and British Museum in London. Some are in the safekeeping of individual collectors.

Famous painter Xiao Yun of the late Ming and early Qing dynasties once copied Ma's works and left behind the *Illustration of Songs Collected in Chen*, which is kept in the Palace Museum of Taipei. Between the fourth and tenth year of Qianlong (1739-1745), the emperor himself and officials in charge of imperial edicts and mandates copied out the whole *Book of Poetry* while imperial painters imitated Ma's illustrations, resulting in a complete *Illustrated Book of Poetry in the Emperor's Handwriting* in 30 volumes, which is kept in the Palace Museum of Taipei.

The 51 poems included in this anthology are all representative pieces from *The Book of Poetry*. Most selected drawings are art curiosities by renowned painters of the previous dynasties, conducive to better understanding of the poems as well as their poetic sentiment.

序 言

◎刘奉文

《诗经》是中国第一部诗歌总集，成书的时间大约在春秋中叶，也就是公元前6世纪左右，与古希腊的《荷马史诗》年代大体相当。初期叫做《诗》、《诗三百》或《三百篇》，到西汉（前206–公元25）时期被尊崇为儒家经典，与《书》、《礼》、《乐》、《易》、《春秋》合称为“六经”。

一般认为《诗经》的编者是中国古代教育家孔子。汉代史学家司马迁在《史记》中说：在孔子之前，“诗”有三千余篇，到孔子时经过他的筛选，只留305篇，与其余“五经”作为教授弟子的教材。

汉代传授《诗经》的一共有“齐、鲁、韩、毛”四家，后来“齐、鲁、韩”三家先后失传，只有“毛诗”流传到现在，就是我们今天通用的版本，所以，后世又称《诗经》为《毛诗》。

《诗经》里所收的诗歌大约是公元前11世纪（西周初年）至公元前6世纪(春秋中叶)前后，约有五六百年间的作品，距今约2500年左右。

《诗经》里的作品，最初产生于甘肃、陕西、山西、河北、河南、山东、湖北等地，据说，周王朝派专人到各地区去采集或征集作品，叫“采诗”，然后献给朝廷。

除此之外，据说也有一些作品是由公卿和士大夫贡献给周天子的。这些作品再由宫廷乐官配上乐谱，唱给周天子听。

《诗经》分为“风”、“雅”、“颂”三部分，“风”包括“ 周南”、“召南”、“邶风”、“鄘风”、“卫风”、“王风”、“郑风”、“齐风”、“魏风”、“唐风”、“秦风”、“陈风”、“桧风”、“曹风”、“豳风” 等十五国风，属于地方曲调，主要是黄河流域，也包括部分长江和汉水流域的民歌，共计160篇；“雅”分为 “小雅”与“大雅”，多数是贵族的作品，属于朝廷的“正乐”，只有“小雅”里的部分作品来自民间，共计105篇；“颂”分为“周颂”、“鲁颂”和“商颂”， 基本是宫廷用于祭祀的歌词，共计40篇。总计305篇。

《诗经》里的作品以抒情诗为主流，兼有叙事诗、讽刺诗、歌谣等形式。

《诗经》内容丰富，包括周代社会生活的方方面面，反映出人民大众反对战争和徭役，反对压迫，歌颂爱情，向往自由的精神。所以说，《诗经》既是文学作品，也是研究中国古代社会、中国古代历史的重要历史资料。

在艺术手法上，《诗经》运用了赋、比、兴的表现手法，具有很高的艺术成就，对后世文学创作产生了深远的影响。

《诗经》是中国文学史、也是世界文学史上的一部不朽的著作，是人类文化长河里的一颗璀璨的明珠。

本书选取了《诗经》里的51首诗歌，都是《诗经》中具有代表性的作品。

由于《诗经》的地位尊崇，所以，中国历史上为《诗经》配图或者以《诗经》为题材进行的艺术创作由来已久，流传下来的美术作品，以南宋(1127−1279)高宗书写文本、由著名画家马和之绘画的《诗经图》最具影响。明末清初的著名画家萧云从就曾临摹过马和之的作品，传世有《陈风图》，藏于中国台北故宫博物院。乾隆四至十年(1739−1745)，清高宗与词臣陆续书写了《诗经》全文，命宫廷画师临摹宫廷里收藏的马和之绘本《毛诗图》，补充其不足，成为一部完整的《御笔诗经全图书画合璧》，一共洋洋30巨册，今藏中国台北故宫博物院。传世的马和之款《诗经图》，现在分别收藏于国内外博物馆、图书馆以及个人手中，包括北京故宫博物院、上海博物馆、辽宁省博物馆、台北故宫博物院、广西壮族自治区博物馆、美国波士顿美术馆、美国大都会美术馆、英国大英博物馆等都有部分收藏。

本书所选绘画作品大多出自历代画师名家之手，也是不可多得的艺术珍品，对于理解《诗经》的内容，体会作品的意境都会非常有帮助。

结廬次江干江田多樹
林秋来讀楚騷痛飲無
虚日　岡奉
恒石先生大教并題博
正蘭陵後學蕭晨

COOING AND WOOING

By riverside a pair
　Of turtledoves are cooing;
There's a good maiden fair
　Whom a young man is wooing.

Water flows left and right
　Of cress long here, short there;
The youth yearns day and ningt
　For the good maiden fair.

His yearning grows so strong,
　He cannot fall asleep,
But tosses all night long,
　So deep in love, so deep!

Now gather left and right
　Cress long or short and tender!
O lute, play music light
　For the fiancee so slender!

Feast friends at left and right
　On cresses cooked tender!
O bells and drums, delight
　The bride so sweet and slender!

guān jū
关雎

guān guān jū jiū, zài hé zhī zhōu。
关关雎鸠，在河之洲。
yǎo tiǎo shū nǚ, jūn zǐ hǎo qiú。
窈窕淑女，君子好逑。

cēn cī xìng cài, zuǒ yòu liú zhī。
参差荇菜，左右流之。
yǎo tiǎo shū nǚ, wù mèi qiú zhī。
窈窕淑女，寤寐求之。

qiú zhī bù dé, wù mèi sī fú。
求之不得，寤寐思服。
yōu zāi yōu zāi, zhǎn zhuǎn fǎn cè。
悠哉悠哉，辗转反侧。

cēn cī xìng cài, zuǒ yòu cǎi zhī。
参差荇菜，左右采之。
yǎo tiǎo shū nǚ, qín sè yǒu zhī。
窈窕淑女，琴瑟友之。

cēn cī xìng cài, zuǒ yòu mào zhī。
参差荇菜，左右芼之。
yǎo tiǎo shū nǚ, zhōng gǔ lè zhī。
窈窕淑女，钟鼓乐之。

Beauties by Xu Ju-an (1890-1964). Xu of Zhejiang Province, noted for his elegant and easy style, was good at painting figures especially beautiful women in ancient costumes. In this painting the artist meticulously portrayed four beauties in light colors while drawing trees and rocks with freehand brushwork.

四位美貌的少女，一持金枪，一背剑持盒，一手拿拂尘，左侧一位舒袖而立。纵观全画配景，松树、山石全用写意笔墨，设色淡雅，人物绘制工细而不刻板，衣纹的线条表现出女性的曲线美。徐菊庵，浙江人，擅画仕女、人物，画风飘逸秀美。

Beauties by Xu Ju-an

仕女图　徐菊庵　民国（1912—1949）

MUTUAL LONGING

Wife: "I gather the mouse-ear
With a basket to fill.
I miss my husband dear
And leave it empty still."

Man: "The hill I'm climbing up
Has tried and tired my horse.
I'll drink my golden cup
So as to gather force.

"The height I'm climbing up
Has dizzied my horse. I roam
And drink my rhino cup
Lest long I'd think of home.

"I climb the rocky hill;
My wornout horse won't go.
My servant's very ill.
O how great is my woe!"

juǎn ěr
卷 耳

cǎi cǎi juǎn ěr, bù yíng qing kuāng
采 采 卷 耳，不 盈 顷 筐。
jiē wǒ huái rén, zhì bǐ zhōu háng
嗟 我 怀 人，寘 彼 周 行。

zhì bǐ cuī wéi, wǒ mǎ huī tuí
陟 彼 崔 嵬，我 马 虺 隤！
wǒ gū zhuó bǐ jīn léi,
我 姑 酌 彼 金 罍，
wéi yǐ bù yǒng huái
维 以 不 永 怀。

zhì bǐ gāo gāng, wǒ mǎ xuán huáng
陟 彼 高 冈，我 马 玄 黄！
wǒ gū zhuó bǐ sì gōng,
我 姑 酌 彼 兕 觥，
wéi yǐ bù yǒng shāng
维 以 不 永 伤。

zhì bǐ jū yǐ, wǒ mǎ tú yǐ,
陟 彼 砠 矣，我 马 瘏 矣，
wǒ pú pū yǐ! yún hé xū yǐ!
我 仆 痡 矣！云 何 吁 矣！

Plum Tree and Golden Pheasants by Lü Ji (1477-?) of the Ming Dynasty(1368-1644). Lü, good at flower-and-bird drawing, was a representative figure of the school of imperial-court decorative painting. In this picture the artist portrayed with fine brushwork two golden pheasants and several birds perching on a blooming plum tree.

白梅树上，落有谷类禽鸟数只，主干上一锦鸡回头赏羽，下面另一只寻食捉虫，虽然宫廷画略显雷同，但本幅仍是作者的精品画卷。

Plum Tree and Golden Pheasants by Lü Ji

山荣锦鸡图　吕纪　明代（1368—1644）

PLANTAIN GATHERING

We gather plantain seed.
Let's gather it with speed!
We gather plantain ears.
Let's gather them with cheers!

We gather plantain seed.
Let's rub it out with speed!
We gather plantain ears.
Pull by handfuls with cheers!

We gather plantain seed.
Let's fill our skirts with speed!
We gather plantain ears.
Belt up full skirts with cheers!

fú yǐ
芣 苢

cǎi cǎi fú yǐ, bó yán cǎi zhī.
采采芣苢，薄言采之。
cǎi cǎi fú yǐ, bó yán yǒu zhī.
采采芣苢，薄言有之。

cǎi cǎi fú yǐ, bó yán duō zhī.
采采芣苢，薄言掇之。
cǎi cǎi fú yǐ, bó yán luō zhī.
采采芣苢，薄言捋之。

cǎi cǎi fú yǐ, bó yán jié zhī.
采采芣苢，薄言袺之。
cǎi cǎi fú yǐ, bó yán xié zhī.
采采芣苢，薄言襭之。

Flowers by Zou Yigui

花卉图　邹一桂　清代（1616—1911）

Flowers by Zou Yigui (1686-1766) of the Qing Dynasty(1616-1911). Zou of Jiangsu Province was good at painting flowers and plants with fine brushwork. From his contemporary, flower-and-bird painter Yun Shouping, he learned the skill of *mogu* to use the colors directly without first making sketches. In this painting almond blossoms and buds herald the advent of spring.

本幅杏花图，粉红色的花朵、花蕾用浓墨枝条穿插，轻松而脱俗。笔墨俊逸婉转，花色绚丽，春意盎然。邹一桂，清代画家，江苏人，擅长工笔花卉，深得同代花鸟画家恽寿平的没骨法真谛。

I ACCUSE

The path with dew is wet;
Before dawn off I set;
I fear nor dew nor threat.

Who says in sparrow's head
  No beak can pierce the roof?
Who says the man's not wed?
  He jails me without proof.
He can't wed me in jail;
I'm jailed to no avail.

Who says in the rat's head
  No teeth can pierce the wall?
Who says the man's not wed?
  He brings me to judge's hall.
Though brought to judge's hall,
I will not yield at all.

xíng lù
行露

yì yì xíng lù
厌浥行露。
qǐ bù sù yè
岂不夙夜，
wèi xíng duō lù
谓行多露？

shuí wèi què wú jiǎo
谁谓雀无角？
hé yǐ chuān wǒ wū
何以穿我屋？
shuí wèi rǔ wú jiā
谁谓女无家？
hé yǐ sù wǒ yù
何以速我狱？
suī sù wǒ yù
虽速我狱，
shì jiā bù zú
室家不足。

shuí wèi shǔ wú yá
谁谓鼠无牙？
hé yǐ chuān wǒ yōng
何以穿我墉？
shuí wèi rǔ wú jiā
谁谓女无家？
hé yǐ sù wǒ sòng
何以速我讼？
suī sù wǒ sòng
虽速我讼，
yì bù rǔ cóng
亦不女从。

Waterfowls in a Lotus Pond

荷塘聚禽图　无款　明代（1368—1644）

Waterfowls in a Lotus Pond, without author's signature, drawn during the Ming Dynasty. The painter portrayed with fine, delicate strokes two white swans swimming in a lotus pond while delineating in rich ink a willow tree on the bank. The picture has a style of the imperial-court decorative painting.

荷花、翠叶、白天鹅，全以淡色写出并与背景拉开距离，柳树则以重墨表现出树的质感，白天鹅从荷花丛中穿过，柳枝上雀鸟姿态各异。整幅画绘制工细，功力深厚，有院体风格。

THE STARLETS

Three or five stars shine bright
Over the eastern gate.
We make haste day and night,
Busy early and late.
Different is our fate.

The starlets shed weak light
With the Pleiades o'erhead.
We make haste day and night,
Carrying sheets of bed:
No other way instead.

xiǎo xīng
小 星

huì bǐ xiǎo xīng
嘒彼小星，
sān wǔ zài dōng
三五在东。
sù sù xiāo zhēng
肃肃宵征，
sù yè zài gōng
夙夜在公。
shí mìng bù tóng
寔命不同！

huì bǐ xiǎo xīng
嘒彼小星，
wéi shēn yǔ mǎo
维参与昴。
sù sù xiāo zhēng
肃肃宵征，
bào qīn yǔ chóu
抱衾与裯。
shí mìng bù yóu
寔命不犹！

Two Steeds in the Shade of a Willow Tree by Hu Cong of the Ming Dynasty. Hu came from Jiangsu Province. The dates of birth and death are unknown. With fine, delicate strokes the artist drew two horses resting in the cool shade of a tree. The horses are very life-like.

画中高大柳树旁斜插一枝桃花，芳香吐艳，树下两匹骏马，姿态不同，形象生动，一马若语，一马静听。此画用笔工细，刻画传神，颇有生趣。
胡聪，生卒年不详，中国江苏人。

Two Steeds in the Shade of a Willow Tree by Hu Cong
柳阴双骏图　胡聪　明代（1368—1644）

A FAREWELL SONG

A pair of swallows fly
With their wings low and high.
You go home in your car;
I see you off afar.
When your car disappears,
Like rain fall down my tears.

A pair of swallows fly;
You go home with a sigh.
When they fly up and down,
I see you leave the town.
When your car disappears,
I stand there long in tears.

A pair of swallows fly,
Their songs heard far and nigh.
You go to your home state;
I see you leave south gate.
When your car disappears.
Deeply grieved, I shed tears.

My faithful sister dear
With feeling e'er sincere,
So gentle and so sweet,
So prudent and discreet!
The thought of our late lord
Strikes our sensitive chord.

yàn yàn
燕燕

yàn yàn yú fēi, cī chí qí yǔ.
燕燕于飞，差池其羽。
zhī zǐ yú guī, yuǎn sòng yú yě.
之子于归，远送于野。
zhān wàng fú jí, qì tì rú yǔ.
瞻望弗及，泣涕如雨。

yàn yàn yú fēi, xié zhī háng zhī.
燕燕于飞，颉之颃之。
zhī zǐ yú guī, yuǎn yú jiāng zhī.
之子于归，远于将之。
zhān wàng fú jí, zhù lì yǐ qì.
瞻望弗及，伫立以泣。

yàn yàn yú fēi, xià shǎng qí yīn.
燕燕于飞，下上其音。
zhī zǐ yú guī, yuǎn sòng yú nán.
之子于归，远送于南。
zhān wàng fú jí, shí láo wǒ xīn.
瞻望弗及，实劳我心。

zhòng shì rén zhǐ, qí xīn sè yuān.
仲氏任只，其心塞渊。
zhōng wēn qiě huì, shū shèn qí shēn.
终温且惠，淑慎其身。
xiān jūn zhī sī, yǐ xù guǎ rén.
“先君之思”，以勖寡人。

Copy of a Song Dynasty painting by Qiu Ying

临宋人画　仇英　明代（1368—1644）

Copy of a Song Dynasty painting by Qiu Ying (1493-1560). Qiu, alias Qiu Shifu, a painter of the Ming Dynasty, was good at copying drawings made during the Southern Song Dynasty. In this copy of a flower-and-bird painting, breaking free from the conventional composition, the artist drew running water meticulously in the lower part while leaving a large blank space on the top left to set off the massiveness of the rock. The images of water, rocks, trees and birds are reminiscent of Song painters' style.

本幅花鸟系作者临写宋人作品，构图新奇，打破以往绘画的上实下虚、四角空白的传统模式，而是以左上大面积虚处理以增强岩石的量感，下方流水绘制精细，动感十足。无论山石、流水、树木、禽鸟，绘制方法皆不失宋人遗风。

仇英（1493—1560），又名仇实父，明代画家。擅长摹古，取法南宋，作品精工典丽。

AN ABANDONED WOMAN

Sun and moon bright,
　　Shed light on earth!
This man in sight
　　Without true worth
Has set his mind
To be unkind.

Sun and moon bright,
　　Cast shade with glee!
This man in sight
　　Would frown at me.
He's set his mind
To leave me behind.

rì yuè
日　月

rì jì yuè zhū
日居月诸，
zhào lín xià tǔ
照临下土。
nǎi rú zhī rén xī
乃如之人兮！
shì bù gǔ chǔ
逝不古处。
hú néng yǒu dìng
胡能有定？
nìng bù wǒ gù
宁不我顾？

rì jì yuè zhū
日居月诸，
xià tǔ shì mào
下土是冒。
nǎi rú zhī rén xī
乃如之人兮！
shì bù xiāng hǎo
逝不相好。
hú néng yǒu dìng
胡能有定？
nìng bù wǒ bào
宁不我报？

Flowers by Zou Yigui

花卉图 邹一桂 清代（1616—1911）

Flowers by Zou Yigui of the Qing Dynasty. In the painting elegant pear blossoms are bathed in bright and clear moonlight. Blooming flowers and full moon were usually regarded in ancient China as the symbol of pleasant time or good things.

"花好月圆"是中国古人形容美好时光，或美好事物的常用名言。此图前景优雅的白梨花，背景圆圆的明月，正是花好月圆的时节。

Sun and moon bright
Rise from the east.
This man in sight
Is worse than beast.
His mind is set
All to forget.

Sun and moon bright
From east appear.
Can I requite
My parents dear?
My mind not set,
Can I forget?

rì ji yuè zhū
日居月诸，
chū zì dōng fāng
出自东方。
nǎi rú zhi rén xi
乃如之人兮！
dé yin wú liáng
德音无良。
hú néng yǒu dìng
胡能有定？
bǐ yě kě wàng
俾也可忘。

rì ji yuè zhū
日居月诸，
dōng fāng zì chū
东方自出。
fù xi mǔ xi
父兮母兮！
xù wǒ bù zú
畜我不卒。
hú néng yǒu dìng
胡能有定？
bào wǒ bù shù
报我不述！

Flowers by Zhao Zhiqian

花卉图 赵之谦 清代（1616—1911）

Flowers by Zhao Zhiqian (1829-1884) of the Qing Dynasty. Zhao came from Shaoxing, Zhejiang Province. He first established his reputation as a calligrapher and epigrapher, and then shifted his interest to painting. A typical literati painter, Zhao applied calligraphic skills in drawing, and as seen in this picture, viewers can easily find the traces of a calligrapher from the use of color and ink and the unique style of inscriptions.

本幅绘画用笔始终贯穿着一个象书法一样“写”的思想，无一笔草草带过，颜色浓丽，寓雅于俗，所作花卉无论色线、墨线、枝干、花朵还是题字的书法、用印，皆统一在同一种笔调之下，融美丑雅俗为一炉。充分体现了中国文人画的特色。

赵之谦（1829—1884），浙江绍兴人，金石书法成就卓著，后植其绘画，挥洒自如，流利活泼。

COMPLAINT OF A SOLDIER

The drums are booming out;
We leap and bound about.
We build walls high and low,
But I should southward go.

We follow Sun Zizhong
To fight with Chen and Song.
I cannot homeward go;
My heart is full of woe.

Where stop and stay our forces
When we have lost our horses?
Where can we find them, please?
They're found among the trees.

Meet or part, live or die;
We made oath, you and I.
When can our hands we hold
And live till we grow old?

Alas! so long we've parted,
Can I live broken-hearted?
Alas! the oath we swore
Can be fulfilled no more.

jī gǔ
击鼓

jī gǔ qí tāng, yǒng yuè yòng bīng.
击鼓其镗，踊跃用兵。
tǔ guó chéng cáo, wǒ dú nán xíng.
土国城漕，我独南行。

cóng sūn zǐ zhòng, píng chén yǔ sòng.
从孙子仲，平陈与宋。
bù wǒ yǐ guī, yōu xīn yǒu chōng.
不我以归，忧心有忡。

yuán jū yuán chǔ? yuán sàng qí mǎ?
爰居爰处？爰丧其马？
yú yǐ qiú zhī? yú lín zhī xià.
于以求之？于林之下。

sǐ shēng qiè kuò, yǔ zǐ chéng yuè.
“死生契阔”，与子成说。
zhí zǐ zhī shǒu, yǔ zǐ xié lǎo.
执子之手，与子偕老。

xū jiē kuò xī, bù wǒ huó xī!
于嗟阔兮，不我活兮！
xū jiē xún xī, bù wǒ shēn xī!
于嗟洵兮，不我信兮！

Copy of a Song Dynasty painting by Qiu Ying

临宋人画　仇英　明代（1368—1644）

Copy of a Song Dynasty painting by Qiu Ying of the Ming Dynasty. With superb skills the painter offered a vivid portrayal of three playing kids with a strong flavor of family life.

三个婴孩在地毯上玩耍，背景一组芭蕉湖石，显然是一个大家族的庭院。本幅画除让我们欣赏画家的绘画美之外，更让我们看到了古代婴儿的体态和生活情景。

TOILERS

It's near dusk, lo!
Why not home go?
It is for you
We're wet with dew.

It's near dusk, lo!
Why not home go?
For you, O Sire,
We toil in mire.

shì wēi
式 微

shì wēi shì wēi
式微，式微，
hú bù guī
胡不归？
wēi jūn zhī gù
微君之故，
hú wéi hū zhōng lù
胡为乎中露？

shì wēi shì wēi
式微，式微，
hú bù guī
胡不归？
wēi jūn zhī gōng
微君之躬，
hú wéi hū ní zhōng
胡为乎泥中？

A Sketch of Flowers and Birds by Lan Tao

杂画　蓝涛　清代（1616—1911）

A Sketch of Flowers and Birds by Lan Tao of the Qing Dynasty. Lan, alias Leiping, came from Qiantang, Zhejiang Province. The dates of birth and death are unknown. He was expert in landscape drawing and flower-and-bird sketching. With both delicate and freehand brushwork, in this picture Lan painted in light colors a cat and a butterfly, which is full of wit and interest.

此幅花鸟小品画用笔工细，兼工带写，施色淡雅。画面中小猫、蝴蝶，似相向嬉戏，幽默诙谐，相映成趣。蓝涛，生卒年不详，号雷坪，浙江钱塘人，擅画山水，兼工花鸟画。

A SHEPHERDESS

A maiden mute and tall
Trysts me at corner wall.
I can find her nowhere;
Perplexed, I scratch my hair.

The maiden fair and mute
Gives me a grass-made lute.
Playing a rosy air,
I'm happier than e'er.

Coming back from the mead.
She gives me a rare reed,
Lovely not for it's rare:
It's given by the fair.

jìng nǚ
静 女

jìng nǚ qí shū
静女其姝，
sì wǒ yú chéng yú
俟我于城隅。
ài ér bù jiàn
爱而不见，
sāo shǒu chí chú
搔首踟蹰。

jìng nǚ qí luán
静女其娈，
yí wǒ tóng guǎn
贻我彤管。
tóng guǎn yǒu wěi
彤管有炜，
yuè yì nǚ měi
说怿女美。

zì mù kuì tí
自牧归荑，
xún měi qiě yì
洵美且异。
fěi nǚ zhī wéi měi
匪女之为美，
měi rén zhī yí
美人之贻。

Retiring Maiden, without author's signature, drawn during the modern times. A girl sitting on a stone is playing a sweet tune on her flute; the music reverberates in the air above a grove of trees. The portrait, painted in a simple but elegant style, has a romantic flavor.

疏林翠叶间，一位娴静俊美的少女倚石而坐，吹奏一首悠扬的笛曲。画面墨淡气雅，设色颇有浪漫主义韵味。

Retiring Maiden

静女　无款　民国（1912—1949）

A DETERMINED WOMAN

A cypress boat
Midstream afloat.
Two tufts of hair o'er his forehead,
He is my mate to whom I'll wed.
I swear I won't change my mind till I'm dead.
Heaven and mother,
Why dont't you understand another?

A cypress boat
By riverside afloat.
Two tufts of hair o'er his forehead,
He is my only mate to whom I'll wed.
I swear I won't change my mind though dead.
Heaven and mother,
Why don't you understand another?

bǎi zhōu
柏舟

fàn bǐ bǎi zhōu
汎彼柏舟，
zài bǐ zhōng hé
在彼中河。
dàn bǐ liǎng máo
髧彼两髦，
shí wéi wǒ yí
实维我仪。
zhī sǐ shǐ mǐ tā
之死矢靡它。
mǔ yě tiān zhǐ
母也天只！
bù liàng rén zhǐ
不谅人只！

fàn bǐ bǎi zhōu
汎彼柏舟，
zài bǐ hé cè
在彼河侧。
dàn bǐ liǎng máo
髧彼两髦，
shí wéi wǒ tè
实维我特。
zhī sǐ shǐ mǐ tè
之死矢靡慝。
mǔ yě tiān zhǐ
母也天只，
bù liàng rén zhǐ
不谅人只！

Cypress Boat by Ma Hezhi
柏舟　马和之　南宋（1127—1279）

Cypress Boat by Ma Hezhi of the Southern Song Dynasty(1127-1279). Ma came from Hangzhou, Zhejiang Province. The dates of birth and death are unknown. He left behind a collection of illustrations to *The Book of Poetry*. This picture, named after a same-titled poem, depicts the poetic setting of boating on a stream in spring.

马和之，生卒年不详，南宋画家，浙江杭州人。传世作品有数卷以《诗经》为题的画卷，画风飘逸，人物造型质朴古拙，山林树石天真烂漫，生动地绘出《诗经》所表达的境界。

MISFORTUNE

The quails together fly;
    The magpies sort in pairs.
She takes an unkind guy
    For brother unawares.

The magpies sort in pairs;
    The quails together fly.
For master unawares
    She takes an unkind guy.

chún zhī bēn bēn
鹑之奔奔

chún zhī bēn bēn
鹑之奔奔，
què zhī jiāng jiāng
鹊之彊彊。
rén zhī wú liáng
人之无良，
wǒ yǐ wéi xiōng
我以为兄。

què zhī jiāng jiāng
鹊之彊彊，
chún zhī bēn bēn
鹑之奔奔。
rén zhī wú liáng
人之无良，
wǒ yǐ wéi jūn
我以为君。

Quails Faithful in Their Pairings by Ma Hezhi

鹑之奔奔　马和之　南宋（1127–1279）

Quails Faithful in Their Pairings by Ma Hezhi of the Southern Song Dynasty. The artist portrayed quails and magpies in pairs with ease and verve. An illustration to a same-titled poem in *The Book of Poetry*, it has a profound moral.

此画构图简洁，笔墨潇洒酣畅，刻画情景生动有趣。树枝上喜鹊双双，水岸边鹌鹑成对，凝眸相视，亲密无间，寓意尤深。

DUCHESS ZHUANG JIANG

The buxom lady's big and tall,
A cape o'er her robe of brocade.
Her father, brothers, husband all
Are dukes or marquis of high grade.

Like lard congealed her skin is tender,
Her fingers like soft blades of reed;
Like larva white her neck is slender,
Her teeth like rows of melon-seed,
Her forehead like a dragonfly's,
Her arched brows curved like a bow.
Ah! dark on white her speaking eyes,
Her cheeks with smiles and dimples glow.

shuò rén
硕人

shuò rén qí qí
硕人其颀，
yì jǐn jiǒng yī
衣锦褧衣。
qí hóu zhī zǐ
齐侯之子，
wèi hóu zhī qī
卫侯之妻。
dōng gōng zhī mèi
东宫之妹，
xíng hóu zhī yí
邢侯之姨，
tán gōng wéi sī
谭公维私。

shǒu rú róu tí
手如柔荑，
fū rú níng zhī
肤如凝脂，
lǐng rú qiú qí
领如蝤蛴，
chǐ rú hù xī
齿如瓠犀，
qín shǒu é méi
螓首蛾眉，
qiǎo xiào qiàn xī
巧笑倩兮，
měi mù pàn xī
美目盼兮。

Figure and Landscape by Luo Pin

人物山水图　罗聘　清代（1616–1911）

Figure and Landscape by Luo Pin (1733-1799) of the Qing Dynasty. Luo, a literati painter, was well versed in landscape, flower-and-bird and figure painting. The picture portrays an old man watching a peach tree in bloom, who's seemingly sighing over the short life of flowers. A diagonal stream divides the tableau into two parts, connected by a bridge on which the old man stands. This ingenious and novel composition shows that the painter wielded his brush with facility and freedom, unrestricted by any conventional method.

水岸孤舟，小桥上，一位长者静看对岸的桃花，象是在慨叹桃花的短暂……。画面用两段式构图，中间用小桥连接，从中可以看出作者作画轻松自在，不受任何“法”的约束。
罗聘（1733–1799），清代画家，出生于文人家庭，山水、花鸟、人物无不精通。

The buxom lady goes along;
She passes outskirts to be wed.
Four steeds run vigorous and strong,
Their bits adorned with trappings red.
Her cab with pheasant-feathered screen
Proceeds to the court in array.
Retire, officials, from the scene!
Leave duke and her without delay!

The Yellow River wide and deep
Rolls northward its jubilant way.
When nets are played out, fishes leap
And splash and throw on reeds much spray.
Richly-dressed maids and warriors keep
Attendance on her bridal day.

shuò rén áo áo
硕人敖敖，
shuì yú nóng jiāo
说于农郊。
sì mǔ yǒu jiāo
四牡有骄，
zhū fén biāo biāo
朱幩镳镳，
dí fú yǐ cháo
翟茀以朝。
dà fū sù tuì
大夫夙退，
wú shǐ jūn láo
无使君劳。

hé shuǐ yáng yáng
河水洋洋，
běi liú guō guō
北流活活。
shī gū huò huò
施罛濊濊，
zhān wěi bō bō
鳣鲔发发，
jiā tǎn jiē jiē
葭菼揭揭，
shù jiāng niè niè
庶姜孽孽，
shù shì yǒu qiè
庶士有朅。

Flowers by Li Shan

花卉图　李鲜　清代（1616—1911）

Flowers by Li Shan (1686-1762) of the Qing Dynasty. Li and seven other contemporary painters were called the Eight Eccentrics of Yangzhou. They all lived in Yangzhou, Jiangsu Province during the reign of Emperor Qianlong and were well-known for breaking new ground in the drawing world when it came to boring its audiences. Li was skilled in flower-and-bird drawing. By integrating painting with calligraphy, the artist fully displayed in this picture the beauty of line and color, which had been pursued by traditional Chinese painting.

本幅作品枝干、树叶、鸣蝉、乃至书法，用笔用墨，同出一辙，将中国画所追求的线条本身的美，充分地展现出来。

李鲜(1686—1762)，清代书画家，为扬州八家之一，擅长花鸟，笔墨纵横驰骋。

A FAITHLESS MAN

A man seemed free from guile;
In trade he wore a smile.
He'd barter cloth for thread;
No, to me he'd be wed.
I saw him cross the ford,
But gave him not my word.
I said by hillside green:
"You have no go-between.
Try to find one, I pray.
In autumn be the day."

I climbed the wall to wait
To see him pass the gate.
I did not see him pass;
My tears streamed down, alas!
When I saw him pass by,
I'd laugh with joy and cry.
Both reed and tortoise shell
Foretold all would be well.
"Come with your cart," I said,
"To you I will be wed."

How fresh were mulberries
With their fruit on the trees!
Beware, O turtledove,
Eat not the fruit of love!
It will intoxicate.
Do not repent too late!
Man may do what he will;
He can atone it still.
No one will e'er condone
The wrong a woman's done.

méng
氓

méng zhī chī chī, bào bù mào sī,
氓之蚩蚩，抱布贸丝，
fěi lái mào sī, lái jí wǒ móu。
匪来贸丝，来即我谋。
sòng zǐ shè qí, zhì yú dùn qiū。
送子涉淇，至于顿丘。
fěi wǒ qiān qī, zǐ wú liáng méi。
匪我愆期，子无良媒。
qiāng zǐ wú nù, qiū yǐ wéi qī。
将子无怒，秋以为期。

chéng bǐ guǐ yuán, yǐ wàng fù guān。
乘彼垝垣，以望复关。
bù jiàn fù guān, qì tì lián lián。
不见复关，泣涕涟涟。
jì jiàn fù guān, zài xiào zài yán。
既见复关，载笑载言。
ěr bǔ ěr shì, tǐ wú jiù yán。
尔卜尔筮，体无咎言。
yǐ ěr jū lái, yǐ wǒ huì qiān。
以尔车来，以我贿迁。

sāng zhī wèi luò, qí yè wò ruò。
桑之未落，其叶沃若。
xū jiē jiū xī, wú shí sāng shèn!
于嗟鸠兮，无食桑葚！
xū jiē nǚ xī, wú yǔ shì dān!
于嗟女兮，无与士耽！
shì zhī dān xī, yóu kě tuō yě;
士之耽兮，犹可说也；
nǚ zhī dān xī, bù kě tuō yě。
女之耽兮，不可说也。

Rabbits Playing in the Snow by Shen Quan (1682-1760) of the Qing Dynasty. Shen from Deqing, Zhejiang Province was expert in flower-and-bird drawing. He had resided in Japan for three years, and thus his painting produced a great impact on contemporary Japanese painters. This picture, made with some kind of Song Dynasty style, portrays a couple of rabbits playing under a snow-clad plum tree in blossom.

几只兔子正在雪中的梅树下玩耍，白梅盛开。其中一只兔子举头向上，好象在疑问那点点的白梅是否也是被冷冷的白雪染成。此图风格有宋代遗风。沈铨(1682—1760)，清代画家，在日本居住三年，对日本人影响很大。

Rabbits Playing in the Snow by Shen Quan

雪中游兔图　沈铨　清代 (1616—1911)

The mulberries appear
With yellow leaves and sear.
E'er since he married me,
I've shared his poverty.
Deserted, from him I part;
The flood has wet my cart.
I have done nothing wrong;
He changes all along.
He's fickle to excess,
Capricious, pitiless.

Three years I was his wife
And led a toilsome life.
Each day I early rose
And late I sought repose.
But he found fault with me
And treated me cruelly.
My brothers who didn't know
Let their jeers at me go.
Mutely I ruminate
And I deplore my fate.

I'd live with him till old;
My grief was not foretold.
The endless stream has shores;
My endless erief e'er pours.
When we were girl and boy,
We'd talk and laugh with joy.
He pledged to me his troth.
Could he forget his oath?
He's forgot what he swore.
Should I say any more?

sāng zhī luò yǐ qí huáng ér yǔn
桑之落矣，其黄而陨。
zì wǒ cú ěr sān suì shí pín
自我徂尔，三岁食贫。
qí shuǐ shāng shāng jiān jū wéi cháng
淇水汤汤，渐车帷裳。
nǚ yě bù shuǎng shì èr qí xíng
女也不爽，士贰其行。
shì yě wǎng jí èr sān qí dé
士也罔极，二三其德。

sān suì wéi fù mǐ shì láo yǐ
三岁为妇，靡室劳矣，
sù xīng yè mèi mǐ yǒu zhāo yǐ
夙兴夜寐，靡有朝矣。
yán jì suì yǐ zhì yú bào yǐ
言既遂矣，至于暴矣。
xiōng dì bù zhī xì qí xiào yǐ
兄弟不知，咥其笑矣。
jìng yán sī zhī gōng zì dào yǐ
静言思之，躬自悼矣。

jí ěr xié lǎo lǎo shǐ wǒ yuàn
及尔偕老，老使我怨。
qí zé yǒu àn xí zé yǒu pàn
淇则有岸，隰则有泮。
zǒng jiǎo zhī yàn yán xiào yàn yàn
总角之宴，言笑晏晏，
xìn shì dàn dàn bù sī qí fǎn
信誓旦旦，不思其反。
fǎn shì bù sī yì yǐ yān zāi
反是不思，亦已焉哉！

Pine, Rocks and Wistaria by Li Shan of the Qing Dynasty. Vines climb up a pine tree, under which the peonies are in full bloom. This is one of the painter's early works made in an exquisite and meticulous way.

一株青松拔地而起，紫藤依松而生，紫藤花垂落下来仿佛能散出一股淡淡的香气，树下牡丹盛开。此画应是作者早年作品，画风工细严谨，但无匠人习气。

Pine, Rocks and Wistaria by Li Shan

松石紫藤图　李鲜　清代（1616—1911）

GIFTS

She throws a quince to me;
I give her a green jade
Not in return, you see,
But to show acquaintance made.

She throws a peach to me;
I give her a white jade
Not in retrun, you see,
But to show friendship made.

She throws a plum to me;
I give her jasper fair
Not in return, you see,
But to show love fore'er.

mù guā
木 瓜

tóu wǒ yǐ mù guā
投我以木瓜，
bào zhī yǐ qióng jū
报之以琼琚。
fěi bào yě
匪报也，
yǒng yǐ wéi hǎo yě
永以为好也。

tóu wǒ yǐ mù táo
投我以木桃，
bào zhī yǐ qióng yáo
报之以琼瑶。
fěi bào yě
匪报也，
yǒng yǐ wéi hǎo yě
永以为好也。

tóu wǒ yǐ mù lǐ
投我以木李，
bào zhī yǐ qióng jiǔ
报之以琼玖。
fěi bào yě
匪报也，
yǒng yǐ wéi hǎo yě
永以为好也。

Going to the Paddy Fields by Xiao Chen of the Qing Dynasty. A farmer drives an ox across a wooden bridge to the fields hidden in mist. The dates of Xiao's birth and death are unknown. Drawing on the experience of his Tang and Song Dynasty predecessors, he was well grounded in painting.

近处堤岸上，几株绿树，枝条秀美，远山消失在浓浓的雾中，农人驱一头牛踏过木桥慢慢前行，踏向飘渺的雾中。

萧晨，清代画家，生卒年不详。画风取法唐宋，工细艳丽，功力深厚。

Going to the Paddy Fields by Xiao Chen

江田种耕图　萧晨　清代（1616–1911）

THE RUINED CAPITAL

The millet drops its head;
The sorghum is in sprout.
Slowly I trudge and tread;
My heart is tossed about.
Those who know me will say
My heart is sad and bleak;
Those who don't know me may
Ask me for what I seek.
O boundless azure sky,
Who's ruined the land and why?

The millet drops its head;
The sorghum in the ear.
Slowly I trudge and tread;
My heart seems drunk and drear.
Those who know me will say

shǔ lí
黍离

bǐ shǔ lí lí
彼黍离离，
bǐ jì zhī miáo
彼稷之苗。
xíng mài mǐ mǐ
行迈靡靡，
zhōng xīn yáo yáo
中心摇摇。
zhī wǒ zhě wèi wǒ xīn yōu
知我者谓我心忧，
bù zhī wǒ zhě wèi wǒ hé qiú
不知我者谓我何求。
yōu yōu cāng tiān
悠悠苍天，
cǐ hé rén zāi
此何人哉！

bǐ shǔ lí lí
彼黍离离，
bǐ jì zhī suì
彼稷之穗。
xíng mài mǐ mǐ
行迈靡靡，
zhōng xīn rú zuì
中心如醉。

Peach, Willow and Mynahs by Ma Yuanyu (1669-1722) of the Qing Dynasty. Ma came from Changshu, Jiangsu Province. Modeling himself on his father Ma Mei, he was good at flower-and-bird drawing. The picture vividly portrays a pair of mynahs nesting on branches.

这幅画描绘早春的景象，两只八哥登落在桃花垂柳间，其中一只精神抖擞，一只却昏昏欲睡，仿佛无论多美的春色都与它无关，一动一静，静谧和谐。
马元驭（1669—1722），清代画家，画风继承其父马眉，功力不逊色于父亲。

Peach, Willow and Mynahs by Ma Yuanyu
桃柳八哥图　马元驭　清代（1616—1911）

My heart is sad and bleak;
Those who don't know me may
Ask me for what I seek.
O boundless azure sky,
Who's ruined the land and why?

The millet drops its head;
The sorghum is in grain.
Slowly I trudge and tread;
My heart seems choked with pain.
Those who know me will say
My heart is sad and bleak;
Those who don't know me may
Ask me for what I seek.
O boundless azure sky,
Who's ruined the land and why?

zhī wǒ zhě wèi wǒ xīn yōu
知我者谓我心忧，
bù zhī wǒ zhě wèi wǒ hé qiú
不知我者谓我何求。
yōu yōu cāng tiān
悠悠苍天，
cǐ hé rén zāi
此何人哉！

bǐ shǔ lí lí
彼黍离离，
bǐ jì zhī shí
彼稷之实。
xíng mài mǐ mǐ
行迈靡靡，
zhōng xīn rú yē
中心如噎。
zhī wǒ zhě wèi wǒ xīn yōu
知我者谓我心忧，
bù zhī wǒ zhě wèi wǒ hé qiú
不知我者谓我何求。
yōu yōu cāng tiān
悠悠苍天，
cǐ hé rén zāi
此何人哉！

Looking Up at Flying Swan Geese

倚艇看鸿图 无款 元代（1206—1368）

Looking Up at Flying Swan Geese, without author's signature, made during the Yuan Dynasty(1206-1368). Reluctant to cooperate with the Yuan's Mongol regime, most scholars of Han nationality had chosen to withdraw from society and lived in solitude. Thus a new school of painting called *yi-pin* (painting of leisure) was created. The picture portraying an old man sitting alone in a boat is an authentic depiction of the hermetic life.

元代时期由于政治影响，大多数汉民族的士大夫、文人不愿与蒙古政权合作，而隐居山林修身养晦，从而又创出了继宋代以后的又一个艺术高峰，被后人称为"逸品"，"逸"即闲适逍遥的意思。本幅绘一长者独坐船头，岸上古松垂阴，正是当时士大夫、文人隐居山林生活的真实写照。

PAST AND PRESENT

The rabbit runs away,
The pheasant in the net.
In my earliest day
For nothing did I fret;
In later years of care
All evils have I met.
O I would sleep fore'er.

The rabbit runs away,
The pheasant in the snare.
In my earliest day

兔爰
tù yuán

yǒu tù yuán yuán
有兔爰爰，
zhì lí yú luó
雉离于罗。
wǒ shēng zhī chū
我生之初，
shàng wú wéi
尚无为；
wǒ shēng zhī hòu
我生之后，
féng cǐ bǎi lí
逢此百罹。
shàng mèi
尚寐，
wú é
无吪！

yǒu tù yuán yuán
有兔爰爰，
zhì lí yú fú
雉离于罦。
wǒ shēng zhī chū
我生之初，

A Hare Gazing at the Moon by Tao Cheng of the Ming Dynasty. Tao, alias Mengxue, styled himself Yunhu Immortal. The dates of birth and death are unknown. Depicting a hare looking up at the moon, the artist created a tranquil, enchanting artistic ambience in the painting.

此图绘高大桂树下一白兔，前左脚提起，仰头凝视明月，造型生动传神。疏竹芳草，溪水潺流，用笔细腻，构图丰满，繁而不乱，意境清幽。

陶成，字孟学，生卒年不详，号云湖仙人。

A Hare Gazing at the Moon by Tao Cheng

蟾宫兔图　陶成　明代（1368—1644）

For nothing did I care;
In later years of ache
I'm in grief and despair.
I'd sleep and never wake.

The rabbit runs away,
The pheasant in the trap.
In my earliest day
I lived without mishap;
But in my later year
All miseries appear.
I'd sleep and never hear.

shàng wú zào
尚无造；
wǒ shēng zhī hòu
我生之后，
féng cǐ bǎi yōu
逢此百忧。
shàng mèi
尚寐，
wú jué
无觉！

yǒu tù yuán yuán
有兔爰爰，
zhì lí yú tóng
雉离于罿。
wǒ shēng zhī chū
我生之初，
shàng wú yōng
尚无庸；
wǒ shēng zhī hòu
我生之后，
féng cǐ bǎi xiōng
逢此百凶。
shàng mèi
尚寐，
wú cōng
无聪！

Day Lily by Li Shan

萱花图　李鱓　清代（1616—1911）

Day Lily by Li Shan of the Qing Dynasty. The day lily is a kind of herb supposed by ancient Chinese to be capable of relieving one of sorrow. The painter inscribed verses on the picture to express his pent-up worries and anxiety.

本幅款题“是色是香皆可画，忘人忧处最难描”。“色”、“香”这些有形、无形对于作者来说都不是难题，唯有心中的忧愁难得一释。这是典型的中国文人画境。

ONE DAY WHEN I SEE HER NOT

To gather vine goes she.
When her I do not see,
One day seems longer than months three.

To gather reed goes she.
When her I do not see,
One day seems long as seasons three.

To gather herbs goes she.
When her I do not see,
One day seems longer than years three.

cǎi gé
采葛

bǐ cǎi gé xī
彼采葛兮。
yī rì bù jiàn
一日不见，
rú sān yuè xī
如三月兮。

bǐ cǎi xiāo xī
彼采萧兮。
yī rì bù jiàn
一日不见，
rú sān qiū xī
如三秋兮。

bǐ cǎi ài xī
彼采艾兮。
yī rì bù jiàn
一日不见，
rú sān suì xī
如三岁兮。

Flowers and Bird by Wang Wu

花鸟图　王武　清代（1616–1911）

Flowers and Bird by Wang Wu (1630-1690) of the Qing Dynasty. A mynah bird is chirping on a willow branch. Wang was well-read in the classics, but had never followed an official career. Legend goes that he often sold his paintings to help out the poor.

红桃、翠柳，一只八哥正在欢喜歌唱，下方春水飘渺，荷叶初放。本幅尤以柳叶绘制得潇洒绚烂，平中生奇，画出“俗”中“雅”。

王武（1630–1690），清代画家。饱读诗书却不涉仕途，常作画济助穷人，品格高尚。

CADET MY DEAR

Cadet my dear,

Dont't leap into my hamlet, please,

Nor break my willow trees!

Not that I care for these;

It is my parents that I fear.

Much as I love you , dear,

How can I not be afraid

Of what my parents might have said!

Cadet my dear,

Dont't leap over my wall, please,

Nor break my mulberries!

Not that I care for these;

qiāng zhòng zǐ
将仲子

qiāng zhòng zǐ xī
将仲子兮！

wú yú wǒ lǐ
无逾我里，

wú zhé wǒ shù qǐ
无折我树杞。

qǐ gǎn ài zhī
岂敢爱之？

wèi wǒ fù mǔ
畏我父母。

zhòng kě huái yě
仲可怀也，

fù mǔ zhī yán
父母之言，

yì kě wèi yě
亦可畏也！

qiāng zhòng zǐ xī
将仲子兮！

wú yú wǒ qiáng
无逾我墙，

wú zhé wǒ shù sāng
无折我树桑。

Amusing Birds in Winter, without author's signature, drawn during the Ming Dynasty. This imperial-court decorative painting depicts bamboos, plum blossoms and pigeons, setting off a scene of tranquility and nonchalance.

本画号无款，但从画风上看应是明代宫廷画，翠竹、白梅、枝下白鸽，此类皆是宫廷绘画的常见元素。画境恬美、富丽。

Amusing Birds in Winter
岁寒禽趣图　无款　明代（1368—1644）

It is my brothers that I fear.

Much as I love you, dear,

How can I not be afraid

Of what my brothers might have said!

Cadet my dear,

Don't leap into my garden, please,

Nor break my sandal trees!

Not that I care for these;

It is my neighbors that I fear.

Much as I love you, dear,

How can I not be afraid

of what my neighbors might have said!

qǐ gǎn ài zhī
岂敢爱之?

wèi wǒ zhū xiōng
畏我诸兄。

zhòng kě huái yě
仲可怀也,

zhū xiōng zhī yán
诸兄之言,

yì kě wèi yě
亦可畏也!

qiāng zhòng zǐ xī
将仲子兮!

wú yú wǒ yuán
无逾我园,

wú zhé wǒ shù tán
无折我树檀。

qǐ gǎn ài zhī
岂敢爱之?

wèi rén zhī duō yán
畏人之多言。

zhòng kě huái yě
仲可怀也,

rén zhī duō yán
人之多言,

yì kě wèi yě
亦可畏也!

Plum Blossoms by Jin Nong

梅花图　金农　清代（1616—1911）

Plum Blossoms by Jin Nong (1687-1736) of the Qing Dynasty. Jin, one of the Eight Eccentrics of Yangzhou, was well-versed in the classics but had never embarked on an official career. His painting has an unconventional grace of its own, representing the artistic conception of keeping away from worldly considerations, which had been pursued by ancient literati painters.

金农（1687—1736），清代画家，扬州八家之一。精通经史，一生布衣，所做作品无不散发着一种清秀典雅、超然物外的美，这正是历代的士大夫、文人画家所追求的画外“画”，即超越所画对象本身而散发出的魅力。

TO A SCHOLAR

Student with collar blue,
How much I long for you!
Though to see you I am not free,
O why don't you send word to me ?

Scholar with belt-stone blue,
How long I think of you!
Though to see you I am not free,
O why don't you come to see me?

I'm pacing up and down
On the wall of the town.
When to see you I am not free,
One day seems like three months to me.

zǐ jīn
子 衿

qīng qīng zǐ jīn
青 青 子 衿，
yōu yōu wǒ xīn
悠 悠 我 心。
zòng wǒ bù wǎng
纵 我 不 往，
zǐ nìng bù sì yīn
子 宁 不 嗣 音？

qīng qīng zǐ pèi
青 青 子 佩，
yōu yōu wǒ sī
悠 悠 我 思。
zòng wǒ bù wǎng
纵 我 不 往，
zǐ nìng bù lái
子 宁 不 来？

tiāo xī tà xī
挑 兮 达 兮，
zài chéng què xī
在 城 阙 兮。
yī rì bù jiàn
一 日 不 见，
rú sān yuè xī
如 三 月 兮！

Flowers by Xiang Shengmo

花卉图　项圣谟　明代（1368—1644）

Flowers by Xiang Shengmo (1597-1658) of the Ming Dynasty. With fine, delicate strokes it portrays a spray of crab-apple blossoms.

浓叶衬白花，一枝海棠自上而下。款题“惜花不忍折”，可见作者爱花、惜花，只有把秀美的海棠花“折”到画中与我们共同分享其美。

RIVERSIDE RENDEZVOUS

The Rivers Zhen and Wei
Overflow on their way.
The lovely lad and lass
Hold in hand fragrant grass.
"Let's look around," says she;
"I've already," says he.
  "Let us go there again!
Beyond the River Wei
The ground is large and people gay."
  Playing together then,
They have a happy hour;

zhēn wěi
溱 洧

zhēn yǔ wěi
溱与洧，
fāng huàn huàn xi
方涣涣兮。
shì yǔ nǚ
士与女，
fāng bǐng jiān xi
方秉蕑兮。
nǚ yuē guān hū
女曰"观乎？"
shì yuē jì cú
士曰"既且。"
qiě wǎng guān hū
"且往观乎。
wěi zhī wài
洧之外，
xún xū qiě lè
洵讦且乐。"
wéi shì yǔ nǚ
维士与女，
yī qí xiāng xuè
伊其相谑，

Egrets in the Shade of a Willow Tree by Lü Ji of the Ming Dynasty. Though drawn by a court painter, it takes on a fresh, serene look.

修长的柳条，点点的绿叶，两只白鸽神情悠闲，上边两只山鸟倒挂在细细的枝条上。本幅虽出自宫廷画家之手，但却抛去了富丽华贵之气，而有一种清新恬淡的田野之风。

Egrets in the Shade of a Willow Tree by Lü Ji

柳阴白鹭图　吕纪　明代（1368—1644）

Each gives the other peony flower.	zèng zhī yǐ sháo yào 赠 之 以 勺 药。
The Rivers Zhen and Wei	zhēn yǔ wěi 溱 与 洧，
Flow crystal-clear;	liú qí qīng yǐ 浏 其 清 矣。
Lad and lass squeeze their way	shì yǔ nǚ 士 与 女，
Through the crowd full of cheer.	yīn qí yíng yǐ 殷 其 盈 矣。
"Let's look around," says she;	nǚ yuē guān hū 女 曰 "观 乎？"
"I've already," says he.	shì yuē jì cú 士 曰 "既 且。"
"Let us go there again!	qiě wǎng guān hū "且 往 观 乎。
Beyond the River Wei	wěi zhī wài 洧 之 外，
The ground is large and people gay."	xún xū qiě lè 洵 訏 且 乐。"
Playing together then,	wéi shì yǔ nǚ 维 士 与 女，
They have a happy hour;	yī qí xiāng xuè 伊 其 相 谑，
Each gives the other peony flower.	zèng zhī yǐ sháo yào 赠 之 以 勺 药。

Puppies in the Shade of Flowers by Hua Yan

花阴乳犬　华喦　清代（1616—1911）

Puppies in the Shade of Flowers by Hua Yan of the Qing Dynasty. With an air of charming naivety, the kitten and two puppies Hua sketched in a style reminiscent of Song Dynasty painters' are full of wit and interest.

画面构图精巧别致，小猫小狗憨态可掬，表情动作意趣横生，可见画家娴熟的艺术技巧和非凡的写生能力。本幅题“仿宋人点笔”，但画面意境比宋人更轻松随意。

NOCTURNAL TRYST

The eastern sun is red;

The maiden like a bloom

Follows me to my room.

The maiden in my room

Follows me to the bed.

The eastern moon is bright;

The maiden I adore

Follows me out of door.

The maiden out of door

Leaves me and goes out of sight.

dōng fāng zhī rì
东方之日

dōng fāng zhī rì xī
东方之日兮，

bǐ shū zhě zǐ
彼姝者子，

zài wǒ shì xī
在我室兮。

zài wǒ shì xī
在我室兮，

lǚ wǒ jí xī
履我即兮。

dōng fāng zhī yuè xī
东方之月兮，

bǐ shū zhě zǐ
彼姝者子，

zài wǒ tà xī
在我闼兮。

zài wǒ tà xī
在我闼兮，

lǚ wǒ fā xī
履我发兮。

Sand Shoal and Mandarin Ducks by Qiu Ying of the Ming Dynasty. The picture portrays a pair of mandarin ducks playing on water, showing that spring is very much in the air.

春水暖暖，一对鸳鸯在水上浮游，夹岸上青草桃花，空中双鸟齐鸣，一幅春意盎然的画卷。

Sand Shoal and Mandarin Ducks by Qiu Ying

沙汀鸳鸯图　仇英　明代（1368—1644）

BEFORE DAWN

Before the east sees dawn,
I put on clothes upside down.
O upside down I put them on,
For orders come from ducal crown.

Before the east is bright,
I take the left sleeve for the right.
I put in left sleeve my right arm,
For orders bring disorder and alarm.

Don't fence with feeble willow tree;
The supervisor stares at me.
He takes night for day and I hate
To be too early or too late.

dōng fāng wèi míng
东方未明

dōng fāng wèi míng, diān dǎo yī cháng.
东方未明，颠倒衣裳。
diān zhī dǎo zhī, zì gōng zhāo zhī.
颠之倒之，自公召之。

dōng fāng wèi xī, diān dǎo cháng yī.
东方未晞，颠倒裳衣。
dǎo zhī diān zhī, zì gōng lìng zhī.
倒之颠之，自公令之。

zhé liǔ fán pǔ, kuáng fū jù jù.
折柳樊圃，狂夫瞿瞿。
bù néng chén yè, bù sù zé mù.
不能辰夜，不夙则莫。

Flowers by Li Shan

花卉图　李鳝　清代（1616—1911）

Flowers by Li Shan of the Qing Dynasty. The chrysanthemum is in bloom in the ninth lunar month when all other flowers have withered. Tao Yuanming, a hermit of the Eastern Jin Dynasty, was well-known for his love of the chrysanthemum. Following an official career full of frustrations for many years, Li eventually chose to leave with some regret. Though Li and Tao lived in different times, similar experiences might make their hearts speak to each other.

菊花开在九月，当其它娇艳的花朵凋零的时候，它绽放在田野。东晋著名的隐士陶渊明以爱菊著世，本画作者李鳝曾几次登仕，但都不欢而散，人虽归江湖，但心中难免遗憾，不由的会与古人的境遇相感。

THE WOODCUTTER'S SONG

Chop, chop our blows on elm-trees go;
On rivershore we pile the wood.
The clear and rippling waters flow.
How can those who nor reap nor sow
Have three hundred sheaves of corn in their place?
How can those who nor hunt nor chase
Have in their courtyard badgers of each race?
Those lords are good
Who do not need work for food!

Chop, chop our blows for wheel-spokes go;
On riverside we pile the wood.
The clear and even waters flow.
How can those who nor reap nor sow

fá tán
伐檀

kǎn kǎn fá tán xī
坎坎伐檀兮，
zhì zhī hé zhī gān xī
寘之河之干兮，
hé shuǐ qīng qiě lián yī
河水清且涟猗。
bù jià bù sè
不稼不穑，
hú qǔ hé sān bǎi chán xī
胡取禾三百廛兮？
bù shòu bù liè
不狩不猎，
hú zhān ěr tíng yǒu xuán huán xī
胡瞻尔庭有县貆兮？
bǐ jūn zǐ xī
彼君子兮，
bù sù cān xī
不素餐兮！

kǎn kǎn fá fú xī
坎坎伐辐兮，
zhì zhī hé zhī cè xī
寘之河之侧兮。
hé shuǐ qīng qiě zhí yī
河水清且直猗。
bù jià bù sè
不稼不穑，

Lotuses by Wang Wen

荷花图　王问　明代（1368—1644）

Lotuses by Wang Wen (1497-1576) of the Ming Dynasty. Lotus leaves, painted in either thin or thick ink on the long scroll, seem to send forth whiffs of delicate fragrance. Wang came from Wuxi, Jiangsu Province. Using the colors directly without first making sketches, he was skilled in drawing the lotus with freehand brushwork.

长长的画卷上浓淡不同的荷叶，润秀的芦苇草，象一部无声的荷塘散文诗，让人心旷神怡。
王问（1497—1576），明代画家，江苏无锡人，擅用大写意没骨法画荷花。

Have three millions of sheaves in their
place?
How can those who nor hunt nor chase
Have in their courtyard games of each
race?
Those lords are good
Who need no work to eat their food!

hú qǔ hé sān bǎi yì xi
胡取禾三百亿兮?
bù shòu bù liè
不狩不猎,
hú zhān ěr tíng yǒu xuán tè xi
胡瞻尔庭有县特兮?
bǐ jūn zǐ xi
彼君子兮,
bù sù shí xi
不素食兮!

Chop, chop our blows for the wheels
go;
At river brink we pile the wood.
The clear and dimpling waters flow.
How can those who nor reap nor sow
Have three hundred ricks of corn in
their place?
How can those who nor hunt nor chase
Have in their courtyard winged games
of each race?
Those lords are good
Who do not have to work for food!

kǎn kǎn fá lún xi
坎坎伐轮兮,
zhì zhī hé zhī chún xi
寘之河之唇兮。
hé shuǐ qīng qiě lún yī
河水清且沦猗。
bù jià bù sè
不稼不穑,
hú qǔ hé sān bǎi qūn xi
胡取禾三百囷兮?
bù shòu bù liè
不狩不猎,
hú zhān ěr tíng yǒu xuán chún xi
胡瞻尔庭有县鹑兮?
bǐ jūn zǐ xi
彼君子兮,
bù sù sūn xi
不素飧兮。

Peach Blossoms and a Bird by Ren Xun

桃花小鸟图　任薰　清代（1616—1911）

Peach Blossoms and a Bird by Ren Xun (1835-1893) of the Qing Dynasty. Ren from Xiaoshan, Zhejiang Province was expert in flower-and-bird painting. With a few strokes the artist graphically depicted the elegance and splendor of peach blossom, which is a perfect delight to the eye.

桃花是花鸟画中的常见题材，最容易画美，也最容易画俗，本幅扇画桃花小鸟虽用笔不多，但绘出了桃花的富贵之气，别具一格。

任薰（1835—1893），清代画家，浙江萧山人，擅长花鸟画，传世作品甚多。

LARGE RAT

Large rat, large rat,
Eat no more millet we grow!
Three years you have grown fat;
No care for us you show.
We'll leave you now, I swear,
For a happier land,
A happier land where
We may have a free hand.

Large rat, large rat,
Eat no more wheat we grow!
Three years you have grown fat;
No kindness to us you show.
We'll leave you now, I swear,
For a happier state,
A happier state where
We can decide our fate.

Large rat, large rat,
Eat no more rice we grow!
Three years you have grown fat;
No rewards to our labor go.
We'll leave you now, I swear,
For a happier plain,
A happier plain where
None will groan or complain.

shuò shǔ
硕鼠

shuò shǔ shuò shǔ wú shí wǒ shǔ
硕鼠硕鼠，无食我黍！
sān suì guàn rǔ mò wǒ kěn gù
三岁贯女，莫我肯顾。
shì jiāng qù rǔ shì bǐ lè tǔ
逝将去女，适彼乐土。
lè tǔ lè tǔ yuán dé wǒ suǒ
乐土乐土，爰得我所！

shuò shǔ shuò shǔ wú shí wǒ mài
硕鼠硕鼠，无食我麦！
sān suì guàn rǔ mò wǒ kěn dé
三岁贯女，莫我肯德。
shì jiāng qù rǔ shì bǐ lè guó
逝将去女，适彼乐国。
lè guó lè guó yuán dé wǒ zhí
乐国乐国，爰得我直！

shuò shǔ shuò shǔ wú shí wǒ miáo
硕鼠硕鼠，无食我苗！
sān suì guàn rǔ mò wǒ kěn láo
三岁贯女，莫我肯劳。
shì jiāng qù rǔ shì bǐ lè jiāo
逝将去女，适彼乐郊。
lè jiāo lè jiāo shuí zhī yǒng háo
乐郊乐郊，谁之永号！

Willow Twigs and a Squirrel by Xu-gu (1823-1896) of the Qing Dynasty. Xu-gu, a monk painter whose original name is Zhu Huairen, was versed in landscape and flower-and-bird painting. The squirrel he drew with light-ink strokes is very life-like.

松鼠是画家虚谷表现较多的题材，此画松鼠翘尾仰首，沿轻曳的垂柳而下，饶有情趣，画家笔法苍劲，尤其松鼠用枯笔皴成，极具蓬松的毛质感。

Willow Twigs and a Squirrel by Xu-gu

柳条松鼠图　虚谷　清代（1616—1911）

THE CRICKET

The cricket chirping in the hall,
　The year will pass away.
The present not enjoyed at all,
　We'll miss the passing day.
Do not enjoy to excess
　But do our duty with delight!
We'll enjoy ourselves none the less
　If we see those at left and right.

The cricket chirping in the hall,
　The year will go away.
The present not enjoyed at all,
　We'll miss the bygone day.
Do not enjoy to excess
　But only to the full extent!
We'll enjoy ourselves none the less
　If we are diligent.

The cricket chirping by the door,
　Our cart stands unemployed.
The year will be no more
　With the days unenjoyed.
Do not enjoy to excess
　But think of hidden sorrow!
We'll enjoy ourselves none the less
　If we think of tomorrow.

xī shuài
蟋蟀

xī shuài zài táng suì yù qí mù
蟋蟀在堂，岁聿其莫。
jīn wǒ bù lè rì yuè qí zhù
今我不乐，日月其除。
wú yǐ tài kāng zhí sī qí jū
无已大康，职思其居。
hào lè wú huāng liáng shì jù jù
好乐无荒，良士瞿瞿。

xī shuài zài táng suì yù qí shì
蟋蟀在堂，岁聿其逝。
jīn wǒ bù lè rì yuè qí mài
今我不乐，日月其迈。
wú yǐ tài kāng zhí sī qí wài
无已大康，职思其外。
hào lè wú huāng liáng shì guì guì
好乐无荒，良士蹶蹶。

xī shuài zài táng yì jū qí xiū
蟋蟀在堂，役车其休。
jīn wǒ bù lè rì yuè qí tāo
今我不乐，日月其慆。
wú yǐ tài kāng zhí sī qí yōu
无已大康，职思其忧。
hào lè wú huāng liáng shì xiū xiū
好乐无荒，良士休休。

The Cricket by Ma Hezhi

蟋蟀　马和之　南宋（1127–1279）

The Cricket by Ma Hezhi of the Southern Song Dynasty. Drawn in a simple and unaffected way, it's an illustration to a same-titled poem in *The Book of Poetry*, which advises people to enjoy life while they can. The philosophy of life expounded in the painting is profound in meaning.

画中主人仰望门外古老的梧桐树，感叹蟋蟀鸣叫起来了，岁末到了，我们不及时欢乐，日子就这样白白过去了。快乐的同时，工作家庭都要顾及，真是不易呀！画面简洁古朴、笔墨松动、意味颇深。

THE PEPPER PLANT

The fruit of pepper plant
Is so luxuriant.
The woman there
Is large beyond compare.
O pepper plant, extend
Your shoots without end!

The pepper plant there stands;
Its fruit will fill our hands.
The woman here
Is large without a peer.
O pepper plant, extend
Your shoots without end!

jiāo liáo
椒 聊

jiāo liáo zhī shí
椒 聊 之 实，
fán yǎn yíng shēng
蕃 衍 盈 升。
bǐ jì zhī zǐ
彼 其 之 子，
shuò dà wú péng
硕 大 无 朋。
jiāo liáo jū
椒 聊 且！
yuǎn tiáo jū
远 条 且！

jiāo liáo zhī shí
椒 聊 之 实，
fán yǎn yíng jū
蕃 衍 盈 匊。
bǐ jì zhī zǐ
彼 其 之 子，
shuò dà wú dǔ
硕 大 且 笃。
jiāo liáo jū
椒 聊 且！
yuǎn tiáo jū
远 条 且！

The Pepper Plant by Ma Hezhi

椒聊　马和之　南宋（1127–1279）

The Pepper Plant by Ma Hezhi of the Southern Song Dynasty. Two characters liken the pepper plant to a lady's bounty and essence. In this illustration to a same-titled poem in *The Book of Poetry*, the painter expressed the poetic conception as precisely and tersely as possible.

画面简淡疏朗，用笔简炼文静，画中二人相视交淡，是在赞美一女主人。他们用花椒比喻她的多子，用花椒比喻她的香美。马和之用最纯朴的笔墨语言写出“诗”的纯朴境界。

A WEDDING SONG

The firewood's tightly bound
When in the sky three stars appear.
What evening's coming round
For me to find my bridegroom here!
O he is here! O he is here!
What shall I not do with my dear!

The hay is tightly bound
When o'er the house three stars appear.
What night is coming round
To find this couple here!

chóu móu
绸缪

chóu móu shù xīn
绸缪束薪，
sān xīng zài tiān
三星在天。
jīn xī hé xī
今夕何夕，
jiàn cǐ liáng rén
见此良人？
zǐ xī zǐ xī
子兮子兮，
rú cǐ liáng rén hé
如此良人何？

chóu móu shù chú
绸缪束刍，
sān xīng zài yú
三星在隅。
jīn xī hé xī
今夕何夕，
jiàn cǐ xiè hòu
见此邂逅？

A Wedding Song by Ma Hezhi

绸缪　马和之　南宋（1127—1279）

A Wedding Song by Ma Hezhi of the Southern Song Dynasty. Binding the cut firewood on a wooded hill, a young man cannot wait to be on the way back home to meet his newly married wife. This is an illustration to a same-titled poem in *The Book of Poetry*.

"绸缪"是反映新婚夫妇的爱情，以及内心充满甜蜜欢愉之情感的一首诗歌。画中男子正捆柴草，若有所思，用以表达天已渐晚赶快背柴回家，与新娘相见之意。

O they are here! O they are here!
How lucky to see this couple dear!

The thorns are tightly bound
When o'er the door three stars appear.
What midnight's coming round
For me to find my beauty here!
O she is here ! O she is here!
What shall I not do with my dear?

zǐ xi zǐ xi
子兮子兮，
rú cǐ xiè hòu hé
如此邂逅何？

chóu móu shù chǔ
绸缪束楚，
sān xīng zài hù
三星在户。
jīn xī hé xī
今夕何夕，
jiàn cǐ càn zhě
见此粲者？
zǐ xi zǐ xi
子兮子兮，
rú cǐ càn zhě hé
如此粲者何？

A Hoopoe in a Secluded Bamboo Grove by Zhao Mengfu

幽篁戴胜图　赵孟頫　元代（1206—1368）

A Hoopoe in a Secluded Bamboo Grove by Zhao Mengfu (1254-1322) of the Yuan Dynasty. A hoopoe drawn with fine brushwork rests on a bamboo branch stretching diagonally on the scroll. Zhao, alias Zi-ang, came from Huzhou, Zhejiang Province. A descendant of the Song Dynasty imperial family, he was proficient in painting, calligraphy and music.

幽篁一枝自右下斜伸左上，用笔如削铁般有力而无丝毫燥气，真正写出了竹的“韧性”。主体禽鸟绘得极工细，神采奕奕，不愧为大家之笔。

赵孟頫(1254—1322)，元代书画家，文学家，浙江湖州人，宋代皇室之后。精通音乐，擅鉴赏。书法、绘画成就极高，对后世人影响甚大。

THE PEASANTS' COMPLAINT

Swish, swish sound the plumes of wild geese;
They can't alight on bushy trees.
We must discharge the king's affair.
How can we plant our millet with care?
On what can our parents rely?
O gods in boundless, endless sky,
When can we live in peace? I sigh.

Swish, swish flap the wings of wild geese;
They can't alight on jujube trees.
We must discharge the king's affair.
How can we plant our maize with care?

bǎo yǔ
鸨 羽

sù sù bǎo yǔ
肃肃鸨羽，
jí yú bāo xǔ
集于苞栩。
wáng shì mǐ gǔ
王事靡盬，
bù néng yì jì shǔ
不能蓺稷黍，
fù mǔ hé hù
父母何怙？
yōu yōu cāng tiān
悠悠苍天！
hé qí yǒu suǒ
曷其有所？

sù sù bǎo yì
肃肃鸨翼，
jí yú bāo jí
集于苞棘。
wáng shì mǐ gǔ
王事靡盬，
bù néng yì shǔ jì
不能蓺黍稷，

The Plumes of Wild Geese by Ma Hezhi

鸨羽　马和之　南宋（1127—1279）

The Plumes of Wild Geese by Ma Hezhi of the Southern Song Dynasty. Nesting on the bushy oaks, two wild geese are waiting for the return of their mates. This is an illustration to a same-titled poem in *The Book of Poetry*.

马和之独创的“马蝗描”用笔为其绘制的诗经题材的作品增添一种奇古之气。本图苍苍的树干，童话般的树叶，潺潺的流水营造出了超然世外的境界，两只大雁栖息树上，在等待同伴的归来。

On what can our parents live and rely?

O gods in boundless, endless sky,

Can all this end before I die?

Swish, swish come the rows of wild
geese;

They can't alight on mulberries.

We must discharge the king's affair.

How can we plant our rice with care?

What can our parents have for food?

O Heaven good, O Heaven good!

When can we gain a livelihood?

fù mǔ hé shí
父母何食？

yōu yōu cāng tiān
悠悠苍天！

hé qí yǒu jí
曷其有极？

sù sù bǎo háng
肃肃鸨行，

jí yú bāo sāng
集于苞桑。

wáng shì mǐ gǔ
王事靡盬，

bù néng yì dào liáng
不能蓺稻粱，

fù mǔ hé cháng
父母何尝？

yōu yōu cāng tiān
悠悠苍天！

hé qí yǒu cháng
曷其有常？

Spring Water and Wild Ducks by Ren Renfa (1255-1327) of the Yuan Dynasty. Ren was good at character sketching. In this top-notch artwork blossoming branches, birds and wild ducks painted with delicate strokes are well-arranged.

本图工笔花鸟图，绘制甚工，花卉枝干呈"S"形向上，线条优美，与下方湍急的春水线条形成呼应，凫鸟动感十足，是一幅难得的精品。任仁发（1255—1327），元代画家，擅长人物鞍马题材。

Spring Water and Wild Ducks by Ren Renfa

春水凫鹭图　任仁发　元代（1206—1368）

WHERE IS SHE?

The reeds grow green;
Frosted dew-drops gleam.
Where was she seen?
Beyond the stream.
Upstream I go;
The way's so long.
And downstream, lo!
She's thereamong.

The reeds turn white,
Dew not yet dried.
Where's she so bright?

jiān jiā
蒹葭

jiān jiā cāng cāng
蒹葭苍苍，
bái lù wéi shuāng
白露为霜。
suǒ wèi yī rén
所谓伊人，
zài shuǐ yī fāng
在水一方。
sù huí cóng zhī
溯洄从之，
dào zǔ qiě cháng
道阻且长；
sù yóu cóng zhī
溯游从之，
wǎn zài shuǐ zhōng yāng
宛在水中央。

jiān jiā qī qī
蒹葭萋萋，
bái lù wèi xī
白露未晞。
suǒ wèi yī rén
所谓伊人，

Flowers by Zhao Zhiqian

花卉图　赵之谦　清代（1616—1911）

Flowers by Zhao Zhiqian of the Qing Dynasty. Though he claimed in the inscriptions that it's a copy of Yuan Dynasty painting, Zhao actually imitated Yuan painters' elegance and ease rather than their drawing skills.

本幅作者自题是临元人的作品，但表面看毫无元人面貌，这正是中国文人所追求的境界，临写的不是古人的"貌"而是古人的"心"。正所谓："师心不师迹"。究其一笔一墨所贯穿的精神无不是元人的松秀和清逸。

On the other side.
Upstream I go;
Hard is the way.
And downstream, lo!
She's far away.

zài shuǐ zhī méi
在水之湄。
sù huí cóng zhī
溯洄从之，
dào zǔ qiě jī
道阻且跻；
sù yóu cóng zhī
溯游从之，
wǎn zài shuǐ zhōng chí
宛在水中坻。

The reeds still there,
With frost dews blend.
Where's she so fair?
At river's end.
Upstream I go;
The way does wind.
And downstream, lo!
She's far behind.

jiān jiā cǎi cǎi
蒹葭采采，
bái lù wèi yǐ
白露未已。
suǒ wèi yī rén
所谓伊人，
zài shuǐ zhī sì
在水之涘。
sù huí cóng zhī
溯洄从之，
dào zǔ qiě yòu
道阻且右；
sù yóu cóng zhī
溯游从之，
wǎn zài shuǐ zhōng zhǐ
宛在水中沚。

Flowers by Zou Yigui

花卉图　邹一桂　清代（1616–1911）

Flowers by Zou Yigui of the Qing Dynasty. The painter drew rocks and grass with freehand brushwork while depicting flowers meticulously.

花朵在浓叶的映衬下形成“线”与“面”的交响，山石用大写意手法绘出，使本幅画量感倍增。土坡上的几笔长草颇有几分野趣。

COMRADESHIP

Are you not battle-drest?
Let's share the plate for breast!
We shall go up the line.
Let's make our lances shine!
Your foe is mine.

Are you not battle-drest?
Let's share the coat and vest!
We shall go up the line.
Let's make our halberds shine!
Your job is mine.

Are you not battle-drest?
Let's share the kilt and the rest!
We shall go up the line.
Let's make our armour shine!
We'll march your hand in mine.

wú yī
无 衣

qǐ yuē wú yī
岂 曰 无 衣？
yǔ zǐ tóng páo
与 子 同 袍。
wáng yú xīng shī
王 于 兴 师，
xiū wǒ gē máo
修 我 戈 矛，
yǔ zǐ tóng chóu
与 子 同 仇。

qǐ yuē wú yī
岂 曰 无 衣？
yǔ zǐ tóng zé
与 子 同 泽。
wáng yú xīng shī
王 于 兴 师，
xiū wǒ máo jǐ
修 我 矛 戟，
yǔ zǐ xié zuò
与 子 偕 作！

qǐ yuē wú yī
岂 曰 无 衣？
yǔ zǐ tóng cháng
与 子 同 裳。
wáng yú xīng shī
王 于 兴 师，
xiū wǒ jiǎ bīng
修 我 甲 兵，
yǔ zǐ xié xíng
与 子 偕 行！

Comradeship by Ma Hezhi

无衣　马和之　南宋（1127—1279）

Comradeship by Ma Hezhi of the Southern Song Dynasty. It's an illustration to a same-titled poem in *The Book of Poetry*. The painter portrayed the characters in the poem with a succinct style.

本图中景二人的目光对视是此画的“画眼”，似在说我们合着穿衣裳，国王要起兵了，赶快修好盔甲刀枪，准备上战场吧。画面人物表情生动，衣带线条用笔洗练，不失是画中的精品。

CONTENTMENT

Beneath the door of single beam
　　You can sit and rest at your leisure;
Beside the gently flowing stream
　　You may drink to stay hunger with
　　　pleasure.

If you want to eat fish,
Why must you have bream as you wish?
If you want to be wed,
Why must you have Qi the nobly bred?

If you want to eat fish,
Why must you have carp as you wish?
If you want to be wed,
Why must you have Song the highly
　bred?

héng mén
衡门

héng mén zhī xià,
衡门之下，
kě yǐ qī chí。
可以栖迟。
bì zhī yáng yáng,
泌之洋洋，
kě yǐ lè jī。
可以乐饥。

qǐ qí shí yú,
岂其食鱼，
bì hé zhī fáng?
必河之鲂？
qǐ qí qǔ qī,
岂其娶妻，
bì qí zhī jiāng?
必齐之姜？

qǐ qí shí yú,
岂其食鱼，
bì hé zhī lǐ?
必河之鲤？
bì qí qǔ qī,
岂其娶妻，
bì sòng zhī zǐ?
必宋之子？

Contentment by Ma Hezhi

衡门　马和之　南宋（1127—1279）

Contentment by Ma Hezhi of the Southern Song Dynasty. A man rests at leisure beneath the door of single beam. It's an illustration to a same-titled poem in *The Book of Poetry*.

画中茅草屋用树干支撑，石头当围拦，虽如此简陋，主人却怡然自得地坐在其中。饮清清的溪水一样可以饱肚，衡起一根木头就可以当做门，真是神仙中人。

THE MOON

The moon shines bright;
My love's snow-white.
She looks so cute.
Can I be mute?

The bright moon gleams;
My dear love beams.
Her face so fair,
Can I not care?

The bright moon turns;
With love she burns.
Her hands so fine,
Can I not pine?

yuè chū
月　出

yuè chū jiǎo xi
月出皎兮，
jiǎo rén liǎo xi
佼人僚兮，
shū yǎo jiǎo xi
舒窈纠兮。
láo xīn qiǎo xi
劳心悄兮。

yuè chū hào xi
月出皓兮，
jiǎo rén liǔ xi
佼人懰兮，
shū yǒu shòu xi
舒忧受兮。
láo xīn cǎo xi
劳心慅兮。

yuè chū zhào xi
月出照兮，
jiǎo rén liǎo xi
佼人燎兮，
shū yāo shào xi
舒夭绍兮。
láo xīn cǎn xi
劳心惨兮。

The Moon by Ma Hezhi

月出　马和之　南宋（1127—1279）

The Moon by Ma Hezhi of the Southern Song Dynasty. A rising moon illuminates a pavilion in which a young man stands all by himself. It's an illustration to a same-titled poem in *The Book of Poetry*. Though not directly depicting the moon and the man's sweetheart he pines for, this drawing accurately expresses the character's thoughts and sentiments.

主人在高高的楼阁上，瞭望着美丽的月光，月光照在他的意中人身上，是那么优美，步伐又是那么的轻盈活泼，他的心突突地跳个不停……。画面并没直接画出月亮和淑女，反而留出了大面积的空白，正是这空白准确地表达了意味深长的情思。

A MOURNING WIFE

The deceased's white cap seen,
His worn-out face so lean,
I feel a sorrow keen.

Seeing my lord's white dress,
I become comfortless;
I would share his distress.

I see his white cover-knee,
Sorrow is knotted on me,
One with him I would be!

sù guān
素冠

shù jiàn sù guān xi
庶 见 素 冠 兮，
jí rén luán luán xi
棘 人 栾 栾 兮。
láo xīn tuán tuán xi
劳 心 抟 抟 兮。

shù jiàn sù yī xi
庶 见 素 衣 兮，
wǒ xīn shāng bēi xi
我 心 伤 悲 兮。
liáo yǔ zǐ tóng guī xi
聊 与 子 同 归 兮。

shù jiàn sù bì xi
庶 见 素 韠 兮，
wǒ xīn yùn jié xi
我 心 蕴 结 兮。
liáo yǔ zǐ rú yī xi
聊 与 子 如 一 兮。

Lotuses by Chen Hongshou (1598-1652) of the late Ming and early Yuan dynasties. As in his other drawings, Chen displayed his superb skills by imbuing the common lotus flowers and leaves with a sense of mystery and wonder.

陈洪绶的任何一幅作品，无论体裁如何平常，但在他笔下总能绘出一种说不出的奇特效果。本图花朵和荷叶并无任何玄奇之处，但却有强烈的玄奇之感，真是平中见奇的高手。

Lotuses by Chen Hongshou

花鸟图　陈洪绶　明代（1368—1644）

THE EPHEMERA

The ephemera's wings
Like morning robes are bright.
Grief to my heart it brings;
Where will it be at night?

The ephemera's wings
Like rainbow robes are bright.
Grief to my heart it brings;
Where will it rest by night?

The ephemera's hole
Like robe of hemp snow-white.
It brings grief to my soul:
Where may I go tonight?

fú yóu
蜉蝣

fú yóu zhī yǔ, yī cháng chǔ chǔ.
蜉蝣之羽，衣裳楚楚。
xīn zhī yōu yǐ, wū wǒ guī chǔ!
心之忧矣，於我归处！

fú yóu zhī yì, cǎi cǎi yī fú.
蜉蝣之翼，采采衣服。
xīn zhī yōu yǐ, wū wǒ guī xī!
心之忧矣，於我归息！

fú yóu jué yuè, má yī rú xuě.
蜉蝣掘阅，麻衣如雪。
xīn zhī yōu yǐ, wū wǒ guī shuì!
心之忧矣，於我归说！

Flowers, Plants and Butterflies by Wang Chuzhen of the Qing Dynasty. Wang came from Jinan, Shandong Province. The dates of birth and death are unknown. He was skilled in using the colors directly to draw fruits, vegetables and butterflies without first making sketches. Drawing on the technique of Western painting, in this picture Wang portrayed in a riot of color flowers, herbs and a swarm of butterflies, setting off the scenery of spring-time.

画面上花草芬芳，群蝶起舞，鲜丽轻快的色彩渲染出盎然的春意。蔬菜、花草以没骨法画出，群蝶则以不透明的浓艳色彩描绘，技法吸收了西洋画的特色。

王楚珍，生卒年不详。山东济南人，擅画没骨蔬果、虫蝶。

Flowers, Plants and Butterflies by Wang Chuzhen

草花群蝶图　王楚珍　清代（1616–1911）

LIFE OF PEASANTS

In seventh moon Fire Star west goes;
　In ninth to make dress we are told.
In eleventh moon the wind blows;
　In twelfth the weather is cold.
We have no warm garments to wear.
　How can we get through the year?
In the first moon we mend our plough with care;
　In the second our way afield we steer.
Our wives and children take the food
To southern fields; the overseer says, "Good!"

In seventh moon Fire Star west goes;
　In ninth we make dress all day long.

qī yuè
七月

qī yuè liú huǒ
七月流火，
jiǔ yuè shòu yī
九月授衣。
yī zhī rì bì fā
一之日觱发，
èr zhī rì lì liè
二之日栗烈。
wú yī wú hè
无衣无褐，
hé yǐ zú suì
何以卒岁？
sān zhī rì yú sì
三之日于耜，
sì zhī rì jǔ zhǐ
四之日举趾。
tóng wǒ fù zǐ
同我妇子，
yè bǐ nán mǔ
馌彼南亩，
tián jùn zhì xǐ
田畯至喜。

qī yuè liú huǒ
七月流火，
jiǔ yuè shòu yī
九月授衣。

Fields of Billowing Spring Wheat by Yuan Jiang
春畴麦浪　袁江　清代（1616—1911）

Fields of Billowing Spring Wheat by Yuan Jiang (?-1746) of the Qing Dynasty. A couple walks on a path in the fields of billowing wheat, looking forward to a good harvest. Yuan of Yangzhou, Jiangsu Province was a great master noted for his huge portraits of great power. It's rare for him to make such a sketch full of life.

青青的麦田小路上，一妇人抱着婴儿，丈夫欣喜地随其后，前面还跑着一只可爱的小狗，充满对未来收获的憧憬。袁江是清代的界面高手，其作品气势辉煌，如此轻松的小品真是难得一见。

By and by warm spring grows
And golden orioles sing their song.
The lasses take their baskets deep
And go along the small pathways
To gather tender mulberry leaves in heap.
When lengthen vernal days,
They pile in heaps the southernwood.
They are in gloomy mood.
For they will say adieu to maidenhood.

chūn rì zài yáng
春日载阳，
yǒu míng cāng gēng
有鸣仓庚。
nǚ zhí yì kuāng
女执懿筐，
zūn bǐ wēi xíng
遵彼微行，
yuán qiú róu sāng
爰求柔桑。
chūn rì chí chí
春日迟迟，
cǎi fán qí qí
采蘩祁祁。
nǚ xīn shāng bēi
女心伤悲，
dài jí gōng zǐ tóng guī
殆及公子同归。

In seventh moon Fire Star west goes;
In eighth we gather rush and reed.
In silkworm month with axe's blow
We cut mulberry sprigs with speed.
We lop off branches long and high
And bring young tender leaves in.
In seventy moon we hear shrikes cry;

qī yuè liú huǒ
七月流火，
bā yuè huán wěi
八月萑苇。
cán yuè tiāo sāng
蚕月条桑，
qǔ bǐ fǔ qiāng
取彼斧斨。
yǐ fá yuǎn yáng
以伐远扬，
yī bǐ nǚ sāng
猗彼女桑。
qī yuè míng jú
七月鸣鵙，

Flowers by Zhang Sheng
折枝花卉图　章声　清代（1616—1911）

Flowers by Zhang Sheng of the Qing Dynasty. Zhang, alias Zihe, was adept at drawing in a realistic style. On the scroll are displayed different kinds of flowers and grasses sketched in a meticulous way.

折枝花卉图长卷，当据生活中的写生作品而来，各类花草交绘在同一画面，丰富而不繁杂，散发着浓浓的生活气息。
章声，清代人，字子鹤，绘画写实力极强。

In eighth moon we begin to spin.
We ues a bright red dye
And a dark yellow one
To color robes of our lord's son.

In fourth moon grass begins to seed;
In fifth cicadas cry.
In eighth moon to reap we proceed;
In tenth down come leaves dry.
In eleventh moon we go in chase
For wild cats and foxes fleet
To make furs for the sons of noble race.
In the twelfth moon we meet
And manoeuvre with lance and sword.
We keep the smaller boars for our reward
And offer larger ones o'er to our lord.

bā yuè zài jì
八 月 载 绩。
zài xuán zài huáng
载 玄 载 黄，
wǒ zhū kǒng yáng
我 朱 孔 阳，
wéi gōng zǐ cháng
为 公 子 裳。

sì yuè xiù yāo
四 月 秀 葽，
wǔ yuè míng tiáo
五 月 鸣 蜩。
bā yuè qí huò
八 月 其 获，
shí yuè yǔn tuò
十 月 陨 萚。
yī zhī rì yú hé
一 之 日 于 貉，
qǔ bǐ hú lí
取 彼 狐 狸，
wéi gōng zǐ qiú
为 公 子 裘。
èr zhī rì qí tóng
二 之 日 其 同，
zài zuǎn wǔ gōng
载 缵 武 功。
yán sī qí zōng
言 私 其 豵，
xiàn jiān yú gōng
献 豜 于 公。

Plum Tree, Bamboo and Birds by Lü Ji of the Ming Dynasty. It's a classical imperial-court decorative painting, portraying in bright colors a plum tree in blossom and a pair of birds perching on its twisting trunk.

本幅《梅竹山禽图》，构图丰满，颜色华丽。画面上半部梅树老干如盘龙舒展，加之似雪的花朵点缀，厚重而又秀雅，老辣而又生机勃勃，主干上禽鸟蹲住其上，颜色浓重造型工细，是一幅院体花鸟画的典型作品。

吕纪（1477–?），明代画家，擅长花鸟画，是明代院体花鸟画的代表人物。

Plum Tree, Bamboo and Birds by Lü Ji

梅竹山禽图　吕纪　明代（1368–1644）

In fifth moon locusts move their legs;
In sixth the spinner shakes its wings.
In seventh the cricket lays its eggs;
In eighth under the eaves it sings.
In ninth it moves indoors when chilled;
In tenth it enters under the bed.
We clear the corners, chinks are filled,
We smoke the house and rats run in
dread.
We plaster northern window and door
And tell our wives and lad and lass;
The old year will soon be no more.
Let's dwell inside, alas!

wǔ yuè sī zhōng dòng gǔ
五月斯螽动股，
liù yuè suō jī zhèn yǔ
六月莎鸡振羽。
qī yuè zài yě
七月在野，
bā yuè zài yǔ
八月在宇，
jiǔ yuè zài hù
九月在户，
shí yuè xī shuài rù wǒ chuáng xià
十月蟋蟀入我床下。
qióng zhì xūn shǔ
穹窒熏鼠，
sāi xiàng jìn hù
塞向墐户。
jiē wǒ fù zǐ
嗟我妇子，
yuē wéi gǎi suì
曰为改岁，
rù cǐ shì chǔ
入此室处。

In sixth moon we've wild plums and grapes
to eat;
In seventh we cook beans and
mallows nice.
In eighth moon down the dates we beat;
In tenth we reap the rice
And brew the vernal wine,

liù yuè shí yù jí yù
六月食郁及薁，
qī yuè pēng kuí jí shū
七月亨葵及菽。
bā yuè pū zǎo
八月剥枣，
shí yuè huò dào
十月获稻；
wéi cǐ chūn jiǔ
为此春酒，

Lotuses and Mandarin Ducks by Hua Yan of the Qing Dynasty. The painter directly used mellow colors to draw flowers and birds without first making sketches. A hue changes into another in a quite natural way.

该图为没骨法绘写花鸟的精心之作，直接用色笔勾画，笔法柔和，色调过渡自然，荷花神韵十足。

Lotuses and Mandarin Ducks by Hua Yan

荷花鸳鸯图　华喦　清代（1616—1911）

A cordial for the oldest-grown.
In seventh moon we eat melon fine;
In eighth moon the gourds are cut down.
In ninth we gather the hemp-seed;
Of fetid tree we make firewood;
We gather lettuce to feed
Our husbandmen as food.

yǐ jiè méi shòu
以介眉寿。
qī yuè shí guā
七月食瓜，
bā yuè duàn hú
八月断壶，
jiǔ yuè shū jū
九月叔苴，
cǎi tú xīn chū
采荼薪樗，
sì wǒ nóng fū
食我农夫。

In ninth moon we repair the threshing-floor;
In tenth we bring in harvest clean;
The millet sown early and late are put in store,
And wheat and hemp, paddy and bean.
There is no rest for husbandmen:
Once harvesting is done, alas!
We're sent to work in lord's house then.
By day for thatch we gather reed and grass;
At night we twist them into ropes,
Then hurry to mend the roofs again,
For we should not abandon the hopes

jiǔ yuè zhù cháng pǔ
九月筑场圃，
shí yuè nà hé jià
十月纳禾稼，
shǔ jì tóng lù
黍稷重穋，
hé má shū mài
禾麻菽麦。
jiē wǒ nóng fū
嗟我农夫！
wǒ jià jì tóng
我稼既同，
shàng rù zhí gōng gōng
上入执宫功：
zhòu ěr yú máo
昼尔于茅，
xiāo ěr suǒ táo
宵尔索绹，
jí qí chéng wū
亟其乘屋，

Flowers by Zou Yigui

花卉图　邹一桂　清代（1616—1911）

Flowers by Zou Yigui of the Qing Dynasty. It portrays a spray of poppy flowers, conveying a sense of tranquility and harmony.

粉红的罂粟花绽放枝上，几屡新叶穿插于花朵和花雷之间，一种静谧和谐的感觉淡淡地散出来，使人眼前一亮。

Of sowing in time our fields with grain.

In the twelfth moon we hew out ice;
In the first moon we store it deep.
In the second we offer early sacrifice
Of garlic, lamb and sheep.
In ninth moon frosty is the weather;
In tenth we sweep and clear the
threshing-floor.
We drink two bottles of wine together
And kill a lamb before the door.
Then we go up
To the hall where
We raise our buffalo-horn cup
And wish our lord to live fore'er.

qí shǐ bō bǎi gǔ
其始播百谷。

èr zhī rì záo bīng chōng chōng
二之日凿冰冲冲，
sān zhī rì nà yú líng yīn
三之日纳于凌阴。
sì zhī rì qí zǎo
四之日其蚤，
xiàn gāo jì jiǔ
献羔祭韭。
jiǔ yuè sù shuāng
九月肃霜，
shí yuè dí cháng
十月涤场。
péng jiǔ sī xiǎng
朋酒斯飨，
yuē shā gāo yáng
曰杀羔羊，
jī bǐ gōng táng
跻彼公堂，
chēng bǐ sì gōng
称彼兕觥，
wàn shòu wú jiāng
万寿无疆！

Figures and Landscape by Luo Pin

人物山水图 罗聘 清代 (1616–1911)

Figures and Landscape by Luo Pin of the Qing Dynasty. Two hermits are having a game of *weiqi* (Chinese go) in a thatched cottage. Pine trees and a stream flowing outside the house add to the beauty and charm of the picture. Luo, a literati painter and one of the Eight Eccentrics of Yangzhou, made a living by the painting brush after his family fell into a decline.

两松后的茅屋内有二高士在对弈，好像能听到“叮叮”的棋子声，他们入神到忘却了屋外清澈的溪水，美丽的松影。

罗聘（1733–1799），扬州八家之一，出生于文人家庭，家道败落后以卖画为生。

COMING BACK FROM THE EASTERN HILLS

To east hills sent away,
Long did I there remain.
Now on my westward way,
There falls a drizzling rain.
Knowing I'll be back from the east,
My heart yearns for the west.
Fighting no more at least,
I'll wear a farmer's vest.
Curled up as silkworm crept
On the mulberry tree,
Beneath my cart alone I slept.
O how it saddened me!

To east hills sent away,
Long did I there remain.
Now on my westward way,
There falls a drizzling rain.
The vine of gourd may clamber
The wall and eaves all o'er;
I may find woodlice in my chamber
And cobwebs across the door;
I may see in paddock deer-track
And glow-worms' fitful light.
Still I long to be back
To see such sorry sight.

dōng shān
东 山

wǒ cú dōng shān, tāo tāo bù guī
我 徂 东 山，慆 慆 不 归。
wǒ lái zì dōng, líng yǔ qí méng
我 来 自 东，零 雨 其 濛。
wǒ dōng yuē guī, wǒ xīn xī bēi
我 东 曰 归，我 心 西 悲。
zhì bǐ cháng yī, wù shì xíng méi
制 彼 裳 衣，勿 士 行 枚。
yuān yuān zhě zhú, zhēng zài sāng yě
蜎 蜎 者 蠋，烝 在 桑 野。
duī bǐ dú sù, yì zài jū xià
敦 彼 独 宿，亦 在 车 下。

wǒ cú dōng shān, tāo tāo bù guī
我 徂 东 山，慆 慆 不 归。
wǒ lái zì dōng, líng yǔ qí méng
我 来 自 东，零 雨 其 濛。
guǒ luǒ zhī shí, yì yì yú yǔ
果 蠃 之 实，亦 施 于 宇。
yī wēi zài shì, xiāo shāo zài hù
伊 威 在 室，蟏 蛸 在 户。
tǐng tuǎn lù cháng, yì yào xiāo xíng
町 畽 鹿 场，熠 耀 宵 行。
bù kě wèi yě? yī kě huái yě!
不 可 畏 也？伊 可 怀 也！

Fishing in an Autumn Stream by Sheng Mao
秋溪钓艇图　盛懋　元代（1206—1368）

Fishing in an Autumn Stream by Sheng Mao of the Yuan Dynasty. Going angling in a boat, the man in the picture seems to be free and easy without a single care in the world. Sheng from Hangzhou, Zhejiang Province styled himself Zhao. The dates of birth and death are unknown. A folk painter, he often portrayed hermetic life in his landscape paintings.

盛懋是元代的民间画家，其山水画多写隐者的生活场景。本图主人公坐船垂钓，空中小鸟划空。山静湖清，道气横生。

To east hills sent away,
    Long did I there remain.
Now on my westward way,
    There falls a drizzling rain.
The cranes on ant-hill cry;
    My wife in cottage room
May sprinkle, sweep and sigh
    For my returning home.
The gourd may still hang high
    Beside the chestnut tree.
O three years have gone by
    Since last she was with me.

wǒ cú dōng shān, tāo tāo bù gui
我徂东山，慆慆不归。
wǒ lái zì dōng, líng yǔ qi méng
我来自东，零雨其濛。
guàn míng yú dié, fù tàn yú shì
鹳鸣于垤，妇叹于室。
sǎ sǎo qióng zhì, wǒ zhēng yù zhì
洒扫穹窒，我征聿至。
yǒu tuán guā kǔ, zhēng zài lì xin
有敦瓜苦，烝在栗薪。
zì wǒ bù jiàn, yú jin sān nián
自我不见，于今三年。

To east hills sent away,
    long did I there remain.
Now on my weatward way,
    There falls a drizzling rain.
The oriole takes flight
    with glinting wings outspread.
I remember on horse bright
    My bride came to be wed.
Her sash by her mother tied,
    She should observe the rite.
Happy was I to meet my bride;
    How happy when my wife's in
        sight!

wǒ cú dōng shān, tāo tāo bù gui
我徂东山，慆慆不归。
wǒ lái zì dōng, líng yǔ qi méng
我来自东，零雨其濛。
cāng gēng yú féi, yì yào qi yǔ
仓庚于飞，熠耀其羽。
zhi zǐ yú gui, huáng bó qi mǎ
之子于归，皇驳其马。
qin jié qi lí, jiǔ shí qi yí
亲结其缡，九十其仪。
qi xin kǒng jiā, qi jiù rú zhi hé
其新孔嘉，其旧如之何？

Flowers by Qian Xuan

八花图　钱选　元代（1206—1368）

Flowers by Qian Xuan (1239-1299) of the late Song and early Yuan dynasties. Qian, who advocated following the previous Tang Dynasty tradition and practice, was good at character sketching and flower-and-bird drawing. On this long scroll, the artist, with his meticulous brush strokes, portrayed sprays of blooming flowers in a natural style without any affectation.

本幅花卉图，全用折枝式绘制，设色浓淡适中，用笔顿挫有力，花卉形态自然工整而毫无匠气。钱选（1239—1299），宋末元初画家，主张追寻唐代遗风，擅画花鸟、人物。

TO GUESTS

How gaily call the deer
While grazing in the shade!
I have welcome guests here.
Let lute and pipe be played.
Let offerings appear
And lute and strings vibrate.
If you love me, friends dear,
Help me to rule the State.

How gaily call the deer
While eating southernwood!
I have welcome guests here
Who give advices good.
My people are benign;
My lords will learn from you.
I have delicious wine;
You may enjoy my brew.

How gaily call the deer
Eating grass in the shade!
I have welcome guests here.
Let lute and flute be played.
Play lute and zither fine;
We may enjoy our best.
I have delicious wine
To delight the heart of my
guest.

lù míng
鹿　鸣

yōu yōu lù míng, shí yě zhī píng
呦呦鹿鸣，食野之苹。
wǒ yǒu jiā bīn, gǔ sè chuī shēng
我有嘉宾，鼓瑟吹笙。
chuī shēng gǔ huáng, chéng kuāng shì jiāng
吹笙鼓簧，承筐是将。
rén zhī hào wǒ, shì wǒ zhōu háng
人之好我，示我周行。

yōu yōu lù míng, shí yě zhī hāo
呦呦鹿鸣，食野之蒿。
wǒ yǒu jiā bīn, dé yīn kǒng zhāo
我有嘉宾，德音孔昭。
shì mín bù tiāo, jūn zǐ shì zé shì xiào
视民不恌，君子是则是效。
wǒ yǒu zhǐ jiǔ, jiā bīn shì yàn yǐ áo
我有旨酒，嘉宾式燕以敖。

yōu yōu lù míng, shí yě zhī qín
呦呦鹿鸣，食野之芩。
wǒ yǒu jiā bīn, gǔ sè gǔ qín
我有嘉宾，鼓瑟鼓琴。
gǔ sè gǔ qín, hé lè qiě dān
鼓瑟鼓琴，和乐且湛。
wǒ yǒu zhǐ jiǔ, yǐ yàn lè jiā bīn zhī xīn
我有旨酒，以燕乐嘉宾之心。

To Guests by Ma Hezhi

鹿鸣　马和之　南宋（1127—1279）

To Guests by Ma Hezhi of the Southern Song Dynasty. The drawing gives a meticulous description of the scene of a feast portrayed in a same-titled poem in *The Book of Poetry*.

这是描绘《鹿鸣》诗中大宴宾客的一幅画面，从画中可直观感受到主人家里宾客满堂、鼓瑟吹笙、热闹纷繁的场面。画幅不大，但画中数十人物形象各异、造型精准，衣纹绘制得一丝不苟，可见作者用功不少。

WE GATHER FERN

We gather fern
　　Which springs up here.
Why not return
　　Now ends the year?
We left dear ones
To fight the Huns.
We wake all night:
The Huns cause fright.

We gather fern
　　So tender here.
Why not return?
　　My heart feels drear.
Hard pressed by thirst
And hunger worst,
My heart is burning
For home I'm yearning.
Far from home, how
To send word now?

We gather fern
　　Which grows tough here.
Why not return?
　　The tenth month's near.
The war not won,
　　We cannot rest.
Consoled by none,
　　We feel distressed.

cǎi wēi
采　薇

cǎi wēi cǎi wēi, wēi yì zuò zhǐ.
采薇采薇，薇亦作止。
yuē guī yuē guī, suì yì mù zhǐ.
曰归曰归，岁亦莫止。
mǐ shì mǐ jiā, xiǎn yǔn zhī gù;
靡室靡家，猃狁之故；
bù huáng qǐ jū, xiǎn yǔn zhī gù.
不遑启居，猃狁之故。

cǎi wēi cǎi wēi, wēi yì róu zhǐ.
采薇采薇，薇亦柔止。
yuē guī yuē guī, xīn yì yōu zhǐ.
曰归曰归，心亦忧止。
yōu xīn liè liè, zài jī zài kě.
忧心烈烈，载饥载渴。
wǒ shù wèi dìng, mǐ shǐ guī pìn.
我戍未定，靡使归聘。

cǎi wēi cǎi wēi, wēi yì gāng zhǐ.
采薇采薇，薇亦刚止。
yuē guī yuē guī, suì yì yáng zhǐ.
曰归曰归，岁亦阳止。
wáng shì mǐ gǔ, bù huáng qǐ chǔ.
王事靡盬，不遑启处。
yōu xīn kǒng jiù, wǒ xíng bù lài.
忧心孔疚，我行不来。

We Gather Fern by Ma Hezhi

采薇　马和之　南宋（1127–1279）

We Gather Fern by Ma Hezhi of the Southern Song Dynasty. An illustration to a same-titled poem in *The Book of Poetry*, it portrays the returning troops after a long, tiring expedition.

"采薇"是描绘征战归来的士兵所赋的诗，反映了士兵经过战争后的生活和内心感受。本章抒发归途遇雪，忍饥受渴的辛苦和悲伤，此画即描绘这一场景。画面笔法简劲飘逸，主次分明，一目了然。

How gorgeous are
The cherry flowers!
How great the car
Of lord of ours!
It's driven by
Four horses nice.
We can't but hie
In one month thrice.

Driven by four
Horses alined,
Our lord before,
We march behind.
Four horses neigh,
Quiver and bow
Reaby each day
To fight the foe.

When I left here,
Willows shed tear.
I come back now,
Snow bends the bough.
Long, long the way;
Hard, hard the day.
Hunger and thirst
Press me the worst.
My grief o'erflows.
Who knows? Who knows?

bǐ ěr wéi hé wéi cháng zhī huā
彼尔维何？维常之华。
bǐ lù sī hé jūn zǐ zhī jū
彼路斯何？君子之车。
róng jū jì jià sì mǔ yè yè
戎车既驾，四牡业业。
qǐ gǎn dìng jū yī yuè sān jié
岂敢定居，一月三捷。

jià bǐ sì mǔ sì mǔ kuí kuí
驾彼四牡，四牡骙骙，
jūn zǐ suǒ yī xiǎo rén suǒ féi
君子所依，小人所腓。
sì mǔ yì yì xiàng mǐ yú fú
四牡翼翼，象弭鱼服。
qǐ bù rì jiè xiǎn yǔn kǒng jí
岂不日戒？猃狁孔棘。

xī wǒ wǎng yǐ yáng liǔ yī yī
昔我往矣，杨柳依依。
jīn wǒ lái sī yù xuě fēi fēi
今我来思，雨雪霏霏。
xíng dào chí chí zǎi kě zǎi jī
行道迟迟，载渴载饥。
wǒ xīn shāng bēi mò zhī wǒ āi
我心伤悲，莫知我哀！

Rowing on a Lake Flanked with Autumn Trees by Sheng Mao
秋林放艇图　盛懋　元代（1206—1368）

Rowing on a Lake Flanked with Autumn Trees by Sheng Mao of the Yuan Dynasty. It depicts a vast lake shrouded in mist. An old man is taking a rest in his boat berthed at the lakeside while a lad is paddling on the lake. Trees and rocks on the bank are drawn with bold, vigorous strokes of brushwork.

画面曲岸清溪，疏林远山，湖面宽阔浩渺。水面有两舟，一长者岸边倚舟而憩，一青年划舟由远及近，动感极强，树石笔法圆劲，率真自然。
盛懋，生卒年不详，字昭，临安（今杭州）人。

LONGEVITY

Plants grow on southern hill
And on northern grows grass.
Enjoy your fill,
Men of first class.
May you live long
Among the throng!

In south grow mulberries
And in north poplars straight.
Enjoy if you please,
Glory of the State.
May you live long
Among the throng!

Plums grow on southern hill;
On northern medlar trees.
Enjoy your fill,
Lord, as you please.

nán shān yǒu tái
南山有台

nán shān yǒu tái, běi shān yǒu lái
南山有台，北山有莱。
lè zhǐ jūn zǐ, bāng jiā zhī jī
乐只君子，邦家之基。
lè zhǐ jūn zǐ, wàn shòu wú qī
乐只君子，万寿无期！

nán shān yǒu sāng, běi shān yǒu yáng
南山有桑，北山有杨。
lè zhǐ jūn zǐ, bāng jiā zhī guāng
乐只君子，邦家之光。
lè zhǐ jūn zǐ, wàn shòu wú jiāng
乐只君子，万寿无疆！

nán shān yǒu qǐ, běi shān yǒu lǐ
南山有杞，北山有李。
lè zhǐ jūn zǐ, mín zhī fù mǔ
乐只君子，民之父母。

Lofty Southern Hill by Ma Hezhi

节南山之什　马和之　南宋（1127—1279）

Lofty Southern Hill by Ma Hezhi of the Southern Song Dynasty. It's an illustration to a same-titled poem in *The Book of Poetry*. The poem compares the towering, majestic Southern Hill to Master Yin who won the full trust of King You of the Zhou Dynasty and held a key post. However, the domineering, awe-inspiring Yin brought calamity to the kingdom.

此山高，此涧深，此石险，这就是南山。画家表现诗中所说的威风凛凛的尹太师。尹太师身居太师却旷废职务，任用财权，贻祸人民，国家既要灭亡了，而百姓们都希望他能够辅佐天子维持四方。

You're people's friend;
Your fame's no end.

lè zhǐ jūn zǐ, dé yin bù yǐ
乐只君子，德音不已。

Plants grow on southern hill;
  On northern tree on tree.
Enjoy your fill
  Of longevity.
You're a good mate
Of our good State.

nán shān yǒu kǎo, běi shān yǒu niǔ
南山有栲，北山有杻。
lè zhǐ jūn zǐ, xiá bù méi shòu
乐只君子，遐不眉寿。
lè zhǐ jūn zǐ, dé yīn shì mào
乐只君子，德音是茂。

Trees grow on southern hill
  And on northern hill cold.
Enjoy your fill
  And live till old.
O may felicity
Fall to posterity!

nán shān yǒu jǔ, běi shān yǒu yú
南山有枸，北山有楰。
lè zhǐ jūn zǐ, xiá bù huáng gǒu
乐只君子，遐不黄耇。
lè zhǐ jūn zǐ, bǎo ài ěr hòu
乐只君子，保艾尔后。

Deer and Pine by Shen Quan

受天百禄图　沈铨　清代（1616—1911）

Deer and Pine by Shen Quan of the Qing Dynasty. In the picture the painter drew a pair of deer under a pine tree with smooth and vigorous strokes.

此图双鹿居坪临海，仿佛能听到海水的涛声，乌鹊归巢而来，设色沉稳，用笔老辣。
沈铨（1682—?），清代画家，浙江德清人，擅花卉、鸟兽。

GREAT HUNTING

Our chariots strong
　　Have well-matched steeds.
Our train is long;
　　Eastward it speeds.

Our chariots good,
　　Four steeds in front,
Drive to east wood
　　Where we shall hunt.

Our king afield,
　　Flags on display,
With archers skilled
　　Pursues his prey.

He drives four steeds
　　Strong and aglow.
Red-shoed, he leads
　　His lords in row.

jū gōng
车攻

wǒ jū jì gōng, wǒ mǎ jì tóng.
我车既攻，我马既同。
sì mǔ lóng lóng, jià yán cú dōng.
四牡庞庞，驾言徂东。

tián jū jì hǎo, sì mǔ kǒng fù.
田车既好，四牡孔阜。
dōng yǒu fǔ cǎo, jià yán xíng shòu.
东有甫草，驾言行狩。

zhī zǐ yú miáo, xuǎn tú xiāo xiāo.
之子于苗，选徒嚣嚣。
jiàn zhào shè máo, bó shòu yú áo.
建旐设旄，搏兽于敖。

jià bǐ sì mǔ, sì mǔ yì yì.
驾彼四牡，四牡奕奕。
chì fú jīn xì, huì tóng yǒu yì.
赤芾金舄，会同有绎。

Fish and Algae by Ma Yuanyu

琳池鱼藻图　马元驭　清代（1616—1911）

Fish and Algae by Ma Yuanyu of the Qing Dynasty. The artist portrayed in light colors a shoal of fish swimming to and fro in the water. The fish, algae and fallen petals floating on the water are all ingeniously conceived.

飘浮着落英的春水中，一群群鲫鱼穿梭其中，荡起阵阵涟漪。设色极淡，除飘落在水中的几朵红花外，其它几乎全是水墨绘出，构思精巧，意境幽远。

马元驭（1669—1722），江苏常熟人，善花鸟画，笔墨清润。

Strings fit, they choose
Arrows and bows,
Archers in twos
Reap games in rows.

jué shí jì cì, gōng shǐ jì tiáo.
决拾既佽，弓矢既调。

shè fū jì tóng, zhù wǒ jǔ zì.
射夫既同，助我举柴。

Four yellow steeds
Run straight and fit.
Our chariot speeds,
Each shot a hit.

sì huáng jì jià, liǎng cān bù yǐ.
四黄既驾，两骖不猗。

bù shī qí chí, shě shǐ rú pò.
不失其驰，舍矢如破。

Long, long steeds neigh;
Flags float and stream.
Footmen look gay;
With smiles cooks beam.

xiāo xiāo mǎ míng, yōu yōu pèi jīng.
萧萧马鸣，悠悠旆旌。

tú yù bù jīng, dà páo bù yíng.
徒御不惊，大庖不盈。

On backward way
We hear no noise.
What happy day!
How we rejoice!

zhī zǐ yú zhēng, yǒu wén wú shēng.
之子于征，有闻无声。

yǔn yǐ jūn zǐ, zhǎn yě dà chéng!
允矣君子，展也大成！

Reed and Wild Geese by Bian Shoumin

芦雁图　边寿民　清代（1616–1911）

Reed and Wild Geese by Bian Shoumin (1684-1752) of the Qing Dynasty. The painter drew a pair of wild geese playing on water with freehand brushwork to create a fresh, refined artistic ambience.

两只大雁浮游水面，一只潜入水中，一只摆羽高鸣，大雁的姿态作者用大写意笔法描绘出来，头、颈、翅膀一笔画成，利用水与墨的自然浸润形成转折，并不在意写实的形体而追求提炼过的意境形象。
边寿民（1684–1752），清代扬州画家，擅画芦苇大雁。

THE CRANE CRIES

In the marsh the crane cries;
Her voice is heard for miles.
Hid in the deep fish lies
Or it swims by the isles.
Pleasant a garden's made
By sandal trees standing still
And small trees in their shade.
Stones from another hill
May be used to polish jade.

In the marsh the crane cries;
Her voice is heard on high.

hè míng
鹤鸣

hè míng yú jiǔ gāo
鹤鸣于九皋，
shēng wén yú yě
声闻于野。
yú qián zài yuān
鱼潜在渊，
huò zài yú zhǔ
或在于渚。
lè bǐ zhī yuán
乐彼之园，
yuán yǒu shù tán
爰有树檀，
qí xià wéi tuò
其下维萚。
tā shān zhī shí
他山之石，
kě yǐ wéi cuò
可以为错。

hè míng yú jiǔ gāo
鹤鸣于九皋，
shēng wén yú tiān
声闻于天。

Cranes and Pine by Shen Quan of the Qing Dynasty. Symbolizing longevity and prosperity in ancient China, the pine and crane became the favorite subjects of the painter. Drawn in a style reminiscent of Song Dynasty painters', it's a rare freehand brushwork painting of Shen.

"松"、"鹤"在人们心目中是一种清高坚毅、吉祥长寿的象征，故画家多喜用松鹤为题材作画。本幅清代画家沈铨所绘松鹤图，二鹤立画中偏左，构图沉稳，笔力浑厚，是沈铨作品中较少的写意精品。

Cranes and Pine by Shen Quan

松鹤图　沈铨　清代（1616—1911）

By the isle the fish lies

Or in the deep near-by.

Pleasant the garden in our eyes

Where sandal trees stand still

And paper mulberries ’neath them.

Stones from another hill

May be used to polish gem.

yú zài yú zhǔ
鱼在于渚，

huò qiǎn zài yuān
或潜在渊。

lè bǐ zhī yuán
乐彼之园，

yuán yǒu shù tán
爰有树檀，

qí xià wéi gǔ
其下维榖。

tā shān zhī shí
他山之石，

kě yǐ gōng yù
可以攻玉。

Flowers by Chen Hongshou of the Ming Dynasty. In the painting rocks of grotesque shapes and appearances at the bottom serve as foils to set off magnolia and peony flowers painted in bright colors.

本画的玉兰花、牡丹花均在深的背景和浓黑的枝叶中脱颖而出。玉兰花蜿蜒曲折的造型与下方的山石形成呼应，画面气息奇古怪诞，是陈洪绶的风格之作。

Flowers by Chen Hongshou

花鸟图　陈洪绶　明代（1368—1644）

REFLECTIONS

Small is the cooing dove,
But it can fly above.
My heart feels sad and drear,
Missing my parents dear.
Till daybreak I can't sleep,
Lost so long in thoughts deep.

Those who are grave and wise,
　　In drinking won't get drunk;
But those who have dull eyes
　　In drinking will be sunk.
From drinking be restrained.
What's lost can't be regained.

There are beans in the plain;
People gather their grain.
The insect has young ones;
　　The sphex bears them away.
So teach and train your sons
　　Lest they should go astray.

xiǎo wǎn
小宛

wǎn bǐ míng jiū, hàn fēi lì tiān.
宛彼鸣鸠，翰飞戾天。
wǒ xīn yōu shāng, niàn xī xiān rén.
我心忧伤，念昔先人。
míng fā bù mèi, yǒu huái èr rén.
明发不寐，有怀二人。

rén zhī zhāi shèng, yǐn jiǔ wēn kè.
人之齐圣，饮酒温克。
bǐ hūn bù zhī, yī zuì rì fù.
彼昏不知，壹醉日富。
gè jìng ěr yí, tiān mìng bù yòu.
各敬尔仪，天命不又。

zhōng yuán yǒu shū, shù mín cǎi zhī.
中原有菽，庶民采之。
míng líng yǒu zǐ, guǒ luǒ fù zhī.
螟蛉有子，蜾蠃负之。
jiào huì ěr zǐ, shì gǔ sì zhī.
教诲尔子，式穀似之。

Reflections by Ma Hezhi

小宛　马和之　南宋（1127—1279）

Reflections by Ma Hezhi of the Southern Song Dynasty. A man sitting in a thatched cottage is looking up at wild geese in flight. It's an illustration to a same-titled poem in *The Book of Poetry*.

一座草庐倚山傍水掩映在疏林茂竹之间，空中雁儿飞翔，庐内之人极目远眺。此图茅屋修竹全用细笔，细而不碎，奇古之气扑面而来。

The wagtails wing their ways
　　And twittering they're gone.
Advancing are my days;
　　Your months are going on.
Early to rise and late to bed!
Don't disgrace those by whom
　you're bred!

The greenbeaks on their tour
　　Peck grain in the stack-yard.
I am lonely and poor,
　　Unfit for working hard.
I go out to divine
How can I not decline.

Precarious, ill at ease,
As if perched on trees;
Careful lest I should ail
On the brink of a vale;
I tremble twice or thrice
As if treading on thin ice.

dì bǐ jǐ lìng zài fēi zài míng
题彼脊令，载飞载鸣。
wǒ rì sī mài ér yuè sī zhēng
我日斯迈，而月斯征。
sù xīng yè mèi wú tiǎn ěr suǒ shēng
夙兴夜寐，无忝尔所生。

jiāo jiāo sāng hù shuài cháng zhuó sù
交交桑扈，率场啄粟。
āi wǒ tiǎn guǎ yí àn yí yù
哀我填寡，宜岸宜狱。
wò sù chū bǔ zì hé néng gǔ
握粟出卜，自何能穀？

wēn wēn gōng rén rú jí yú mù
温温恭人，如集于木。
zhuì zhuì xiǎo xīn rú lín yú gǔ
惴惴小心，如临于谷。
zhàn zhàn jīng jīng rú lǚ bó bīng
战战兢兢，如履薄冰。

Flowers by Zou Yigui

花卉图　邹一桂　清代（1616—1911）

Flowers by Zou Yigui of the Qing Dynasty. The lilies drawn in a fresh, chaste style seem to send forth a faint, sweet fragrance.

纷纷的百合花叶交错得有条不紊，这种“碎者整之”的画法要诀当是作者认真观察生活的体悟，红黄色的百合花姿态各异，显得格外生动自然。

REVELRY

The guests come with delight
And take place left and right.
In rows arranged the dishes,
Displayed viands and fishes.
The wine is mild and good;
They drink and eat the food.
Bells and drums in their place,
They raise their cups with grace.
The target set on foot,
With bows for them to shoot,
The archers stand in row,
Ready their skill to show.
If the target is hit,
You'll drink a cup for it.

They dance to music sweet
Of flute and to drumbeat.
Rites are performed to please
Our ancestors with ease.
The offerings on hand
Are so full and so grand.
You will be richly blessed,
Sons, grandsons and the rest.

bīn zhī chū yán
宾之初筵

bīn zhī chū yán zuǒ yòu zhì zhì
宾之初筵，左右秩秩。
biān dòu yǒu chǔ yáo hé wéi lǚ
笾豆有楚，殽核维旅。
jiǔ jì hé zhǐ yǐn jiǔ kǒng xié
酒既和旨，饮酒孔偕。
zhōng gǔ jì shè jǔ chóu yì yì
钟鼓既设，举酬逸逸。
dà hóu jì kàng gōng shǐ sī zhāng
大侯既抗，弓矢斯张。
shè fū jì tóng xiàn ěr fā gōng
射夫既同，献尔发功。
fā bǐ yǒu dì yǐ qí ěr jué
发彼有的，以祈尔爵。

yuè wǔ shēng gǔ yuè jì hé zòu
籥舞笙鼓，乐既和奏。
zhēng kàn liè zǔ yǐ qià bǎi lǐ
烝衎烈祖，以洽百礼。
bǎi lǐ jì zhì yǒu rén yǒu lín
百礼既至，有壬有林。
xī ěr chún gǔ zǐ sūn qí dān
锡尔纯嘏，子孙其湛。

Flowers by Xiang Shengmo

花卉图　项圣谟　明代（1368—1644）

Flowers by Xiang Shengmo of the Ming Dynasty. Drawn in a succinct style, it's a most exquisite piece of painting. Living in the last years of the Ming Dynasty and having witnessed its downfall, Xiang expressed his concern over the country and the people through his painting brush. He was most versed in portraying the pine, which conveys the painter's indomitable spirit.

此幅花卉当是作者小品，但“简”而不“单”端庄正直，笔墨精湛，笔笔送到，作者忧国忧民的心情全然流露纸上，不失其不屈不挠的本色。

项圣谟（1597—1658），明末画家，曾亲眼目睹明王朝败亡的场景。一生以画松最精，以寄托坚毅不屈的精神。

Happy is every man.
Let each do what he can.
Each guest shoots with his bow;
The host joins in the row.
Let's fill an empty cup.
When one hits, all cheer up.

qí dān yuē lè, gè zòu ěr néng.
其湛曰乐，各奏尔能。
bīn zài shǒu qiú, shì rén rù yòu.
宾载手仇，室人入又。
zhuó bǐ kāng jué, yǐ zòu ěr shí.
酌彼康爵，以奏尔时。

When guests begin to feast,
They are gentle at least.
When they've not drunk too much,
　　They would observe the rite;
When they have drunk too much,
　　Their deportment is light.
They leave their seats and go
Capering to and fro.
When they've not drunk too much,
　　They are in a good mood;
When they have drunk too much,
　　They're indecent and rude.
When they are deeply drunk,
They know not where they're sunk.

bīn zhī chū yán, wēn wēn qí gōng.
宾之初筵，温温其恭。
qí wèi zuì zhǐ, wēi yí fǎn fǎn.
其未醉止，威仪反反。
yuē jì zuì zhǐ, wēi yí fān fān.
曰既醉止，威仪幡幡。
shě qí zuò qiān, lǚ wǔ xiān xiān.
舍其坐迁，屡舞僊僊。
qí wèi zuì zhǐ, wēi yí yì yì.
其未醉止，威仪抑抑。
yuē jì zuì zhǐ, wēi yí bì bì.
曰既醉止，威仪怭怭。
shì yuē jì zuì, bù zhī qí zhì.
是曰既醉，不知其秩。

When they've drunk their cups dry,
They shout out, brawl and cry.
They put plates upside down;
They dance like funny clown.

bīn jì zuì zhǐ, zài háo zài náo.
宾既醉止，载号载呶。
luàn wǒ biān dòu, lǚ wǔ qī qī.
乱我笾豆，屡舞僛僛。

Lotus by Xie Sun

荷花图　谢荪　清代（1616—1911）

Lotus by Xie Sun of the Qing Dynasty. Xie from Jiangsu Province was good at flower sketching. He portrayed a lotus flower supported by green leaves with fine, delicate strokes. This is an elegant, refreshing sketch.

荷花在荷叶的包裹中展露出来，几株水草随意穿插其间，荷花在绿叶的衬托下显得光彩奕奕。画家线条极工细，连荷叶脉络也一丝不苟地勾写出来，整个画面气静神闲，清气怡人。

谢荪，清代画家，江苏人。擅花卉，为"金陵八家"之一。

When they have drunk wine strong,
They know not right from wrong.
With their cups on one side,
They dance and slip and slide.
If drunk they went away,
The host would happy stay.
But drunk they will not go;
The host is full of woe.
We may drink with delight
If we observe the rite.

shì yuē jì zuì, bù zhī qí yóu.
是曰既醉，不知其邮。
cè biàn zhī é, lǚ wǔ suō suō.
侧弁之俄，屡舞傞傞。
jì zuì ér chū, bìng shòu qí fú.
既醉而出，并受其福。
zuì ér bù chū, shì wèi fá dé.
醉而不出，是谓伐德。
yǐn jiǔ kǒng jiā, wéi qí lìng yí.
饮酒孔嘉，维其令仪。

Whenever people drink,
In drunkenness some sink.
Appoint an inspector
And keep a register.
But drunkards feel no shame;
On others they'll lay blame.
Don't drink any more toast,
Or they will wrong the host.
Do not speak if you could;
Say only what you should.
Don't say like drunkard born
You're a ram without horn.
With three cups you've lost head;
With more you'd be drunk dead.

fán cǐ yǐn jiǔ, huò zuì huò fǒu.
凡此饮酒，或醉或否。
jì lì zhī jiān, huò zuǒ zhī shǐ.
既立之监，或佐之史。
bǐ zuì bù zāng, bù zuì fǎn chǐ.
彼醉不臧，不醉反耻。
shì wù cóng wèi, wú bǐ tài dài.
式勿从谓，无俾大怠。
fěi yán wù yán, fěi yóu wù yǔ.
匪言勿言，匪由勿语。
yóu zuì zhī yán, bǐ chū tóng gǔ.
由醉之言，俾出童羖。
sān jué bù shí, shěn gǎn duō yòu.
三爵不识，矧敢多又。

Bird and Flowers by Ren Xun
花鸟图　任薰　清代（1616–1911）

Bird and Flowers by Ren Xun of the Qing Dynasty. The painter used a riot of color directly to draw the bird, flowers, leaves and branches without first making sketches. The composition is compactly laid out, giving viewers a sense of harmonious beauty.

此画表现出一只小鸟极速飞驰而来即将落到花枝上的一刹那。花朵、枝叶、枝干乃至小鸟全用没骨法写出，笔笔到位，无一丝拖泥带水之感。

THE FISH AMONG THE WEED

The fish among the weed,
Showing large head, swims with speed.
The king in the capital
Drinks happy in the hall.

The fish swims thereamong,
Showing its tail so long.
The king in the capital
Drinks cheerful in the hall.

The fish among the weed
Sheltered by rush and reed,
The king in the capital
Dwells carefree in the hall.

yú zǎo
鱼 藻

yú zài zài zǎo yǒu fén qí shǒu
鱼在在藻，有颁其首。
wáng zài zài hào kǎi lè yǐn jiǔ
王在在镐，岂乐饮酒。

yú zài zài zǎo yǒu shēn qí wěi
鱼在在藻，有莘其尾。
wáng zài zài hào yǐn jiǔ lè kǎi
王在在镐，饮酒乐岂。

yú zài zài zǎo yī yú qí pú
鱼在在藻，依于其蒲。
wáng zài zài hào yǒu nuó qí jū
王在在镐，有那其居。

Goldfish by Xu-gu of the Qing Dynasty. By light-ink and dry-brush strokes the painter drew pine needles and drooping clusters of wistaria flowers overhanging a pond. The frequent use of oblique or adverse force of the brush has lent a rare charm to his paintings.

枯笔写成的松针藤罗悬挂在池塘上面，水中可爱的小金鱼穿梭于渔藻间，逆笔枯墨综合运用，节奏鲜明，质感强烈。

虚谷（1823—1896），本姓朱，清代画家，擅长花鸟画，枯笔、偏锋是他的特色，画风别具一格。

Goldfish by Xu-gu

金鱼图　虚谷　清代（1616—1911）

THREE KINGS OF ZHOU

Gods know on high
What's done below.
We can't rely
On grace they show.
It's hard to retain
The royal crown.
Yin-Shang did reign;
It's overthrown.

Ren, Princess Yin ,
Left Shang's town-wall
To marry in
Zhou's capital.
She wed King Ji,
The best of men.
Then pregnant, she
Gave birth to Wen.

When he was crowned,
Wen served with care
The gods around,
Blessed here and there.
His virtue's great,
Fit head of the state.

dà míng
大明

míng míng zài xià, hè hè zài shàng.
明明在下，赫赫在上。
tiān nán chén sī, bù yì wéi wáng.
天难忱斯，不易维王。
tiān wèi yīn dí, shǐ bù jiā sì fāng.
天位殷適，使不挟四方。

zhì zhòng shì rén, zì bǐ yīn shāng,
挚仲氏任，自彼殷商，
lái jià yú zhōu, yuē pín yú jīng,
来嫁于周，曰嫔于京，
nǎi jí wáng jì, wéi dé zhī xíng.
乃及王季，维德之行。

tài rén yǒu shēn, shēng cǐ wén wáng.
大任有身，生此文王。
wéi cǐ wén wáng, xiǎo xīn yì yì.
维此文王，小心翼翼。
zhāo shì shàng dì, yù huái duō fú.
昭事上帝，聿怀多福。
jué dé bù huí, yǐ shòu fāng guó.
厥德不回，以受方国。

Landscape by Jin Nong

山水图　金农　清代（1616–1911）

Landscape by Jin Nong of the Qing Dynasty. Reed marshes drawn with tiny dots come into focus of the painting, in contrast to the inscriptions above. Several skiffs on the lake have infused vigor into the scene. Overall, though painted in a quite simple way, it is rich in poetic flavor.

用胡椒点画出的芦苇丝几乎成了本幅画的主体，几叶小舟象比赛似的急速前划，船尾翘起的角度表示前进的速度，细观此图，笔法、墨法简单之至，但并无单调感。浓浓的胡椒点与题跋的书法遥相呼应，一幅平湖赛艇图展示眼前。

Heaven above
　　Ruled o'er our fate.
It chose with love
　　For Wen a mate.
On sunny side
　　Of River Wei
Wen found his bride
　　In rich array.

Born in a large state,
　　The celestial bride
And auspicious mate
　　Stood by riverside.
On birdge of boats they met,
Splendor ne'er to forget.

At Heaven's call
　　Wen again wed
In capital
　　Xin nobly-bred.
She bore a son
　　Who should take down,
When victory's won,
　　The royal crown.

tiān jiān zài xià, yǒu mìng jì jí
天监在下，有命既集。
wén wáng chū zài, tiān zuò zhī hé
文王初载，天作之合。
zài hé zhī yáng, zài wèi zhī sì
在洽之阳，在渭之涘。

wén wáng jiā zhǐ, dà bāng yǒu zǐ
文王嘉止，大邦有子。
dà bāng yǒu zǐ, qiàn tiān zhī mèi
大邦有子，俔天之妹。
wén wáng jué xiáng, qīn yíng yú wèi
文王厥祥，亲迎于渭。
zào zhōu wéi liáng, bù xiǎng qí guāng
造舟为梁，不显其光。

yǒu mìng zì tiān, mìng cǐ wén wáng,
有命自天，命此文王，
yú zhōu yú jīng, zuǎn nǚ wéi shēn,
于周于京。缵女维莘，
zhǎng zǐ wéi xíng, dǔ shēng wǔ wáng
长子维行，笃生武王。
bǎo yòu mìng ěr, xiè fá dà shāng
保右命尔，燮伐大商。

Flowers and Birds by Li Shan of the Qing Dynasty. The artist drew the flowers and birds with fine brushwork while showing the shades and texture of rocks by bold, light-ink strokes.

树石花草争晖，小鸟栖枝鸣唱，花鸟笔墨用小写意笔法，风格秀丽柔和，山石皴擦较为粗放，粗中有细，画功颇深。

Flowers and Birds by Li Shan

花鸟图　李鱓　清代（1616—1911）

Shang troops did wield
Stones on hard wood.
Wu vowed afield:
"To us kinghood!
Gods are behind.
Keep your strong mind!"

The field is wide;
War chariots strong.
The steeds we ride
Gallop along.
Our Master Jiang
Assists the king
To overthrow the Shang
Like eagle on the wing.
A morning bright
Displaced the night.

yīn shāng zhī lǚ qí huì rú lín
殷商之旅，其会如林。
shǐ yú mù yě wéi yú hóu xīng
矢于牧野：“维予侯兴。
shàng dì lín rǔ wú èr ěr xīn
上帝临汝，无贰尔心！”

mù yě yáng yáng tán jū huáng huáng
牧野洋洋，檀车煌煌，
sì yuán bāng bāng wéi shī shàng fù
驷騵彭彭。维师尚父，
shí wéi yīng yáng liàng bǐ wǔ wáng
时维鹰扬。凉彼武王。
sì fá dà shāng huì zhāo qīng míng
肆伐大商，会朝清明！

Chrysanthemums by Yun Shouping (1633-1690) of the Qing Dynasty. The painter delineated two chrysanthemums meticulously with smooth and vigorous strokes.

姿态宛然的野菊花倒挂在山涯上，花头向上，像是在展示生命的顽强。恽寿平是没骨法画花卉的高手，但此幅却是笔笔写出山石、枝叶、花瓣，勾勒严谨，笔力老辣，是其难得的一幅精品。

Chrysanthemums by Yun Shouping

菊花图　恽寿平　清代（1616—1911）

THE MIGRATION IN 1325 B.C.

Gourds grow in long, long trains;
Our people grew in the plains.
They moved to Qi from Tu,
Led by old Duke Tan Fu,
And built kilnlike hut and cave
For house they did not have.

Tan Fu took morning ride;
Along the western side
Of River Wei came he
To the foot of Mount Qi;
His wife Jiang came at his right
To find a housing site.

Zhou plain spread at his feet

mián
绵

mián mián guā dié
绵 绵 瓜 瓞。
mín zhī chū shēng
民 之 初 生，
zì tǔ jū qī
自 土 沮 漆。
gǔ gōng dǎn fǔ
古 公 亶 父，
táo fù táo xué
陶 复 陶 穴，
wèi yǒu jiā shì
未 有 家 室。

gǔ gōng dǎn fǔ
古 公 亶 父，
lái zhāo zǒu mǎ
来 朝 走 马；
shuài xī shuǐ hǔ
率 西 水 浒，
zhì yú qí xià
至 于 岐 下。
yuán jí jiāng nǚ
爰 及 姜 女，
yù lái xū yǔ
聿 来 胥 宇。

zhōu yuán wǔ wǔ
周 原 膴 膴，

Green Garden by Shen Zhou

青园图　沈周　明代（1368–1644）

Green Garden by Shen Zhou (1427-1509) of the Ming Dynasty. A hermit is reading in a thatched cottage shaded by slender bamboos and weeping willows, which makes a tranquil, idyllic scene. Shen, alias Shitian, from Suzhou, Jiangsu Province, was expert in landscape, figure and flower-and-bird painting. Deeply influenced by Yuan Dynasty painters Wang Meng and Wu Zhen, he was adept at line drawing with a bald brush. Though many contemporaries vied in counterfeiting his paintings, Shen had never made a fuss but remained cool and collected.

本幅平水石砥上三间小屋，一长者独坐持卷，屋外修篁垂柳，俨然一个山林隐者的镜头。

沈周（1427–1509），号石田，长洲（今江苏苏州）人。能画人物、山水、花鸟，以山水画最为突出。画风融汇宋元，受元代的王蒙、吴镇影响最深，擅用秃笔直写，朴实平易中显示出倔强的个性。沈周为人忠厚，当时仿造其画者甚多，沈周都能泰然处之，是明代画坛上的领袖人物。

With plants and violets sweet.
He asked his men their mind,
And by tortoise shell divined.
He was told there to stay
And build homes rightaway.

They settled at the site
And planned to build left and right.
They divided the ground
And dug ditches around.
From west to east there was no land
But Tan Fu took in hand.

He named two officers
In charge of laborers
To build their houses fine.
They made walls straight with the line

jǐn tú rú yí
堇荼如饴。
yuán shǐ yuán móu
爰始爰谋，
yuán qì wǒ guī
爰契我龟；
yuē zhǐ yuē shí
曰止曰时，
zhù shì yú zī
筑室于兹。

nǎi wèi nǎi zhǐ
迺慰迺止，
nǎi zuǒ nǎi yòu
迺左迺右；
nǎi jiāng nǎi lǐ
迺疆迺理，
nǎi xuān nǎi mǔ
迺宣迺亩。
zì xī cú dōng
自西徂东，
zhōu yuán zhí shì
周爰执事。

nǎi zhào sī kōng
乃召司空，
nǎi zhào sī tú
乃召司徒，
bǐ lì shì jiā
俾立室家。
qí shéng zé zhí
其绳则直，

A Hawk Chasing a Songbird by Wang Yuan (1280-1360) of the Yuan Dynasty. Wang was versed in flower-and-bird drawing and bamboo painting in ink. In this picture he vividly sketched the fierce eagle and fleeing bird by light-ink strokes.

雄鹰急速追逐苍惶逃走的画眉鸟，为了更好地表现这生动的场面，作者安排画眉鸟从树枝间穿过以增强其惊恐的形象。笔墨处理上勾勒和水墨皴染的方法并用，质感活灵活现。

王渊(1280—1360)，元代画家，擅花鸟、墨竹。

A Hawk Chasing a Songbird by Wang Yuan

鹰逐画眉图　王渊　元代（1206—1368）

And bound the frame-boards tight.	sù bǎn yǐ zài 缩 版 以 载，
A temple rose in sight.	zuò miào yì yì 作 庙 翼 翼。
They brought basketfuls of earth	jū zhī réng réng 捄 之 陾 陾，
And cast it in frames with mirth.	duó zhī hōng hōng 度 之 薨 薨，
Then they beat it with blows	zhù zhī dēng dēng 筑 之 登 登，
And pared the walls in rows.	xuē lǚ píng píng 削 屡 冯 冯。
A hundred walls did rise;	bǎi dǔ jiē xīng 百 堵 皆 兴，
Drums were drowned in their cries.	gāo gǔ fú shèng 鼛 鼓 弗 胜。
They set up city gate;	nǎi lì gāo mén 迺 立 皋 门，
It stood so high and straight.	gāo mén yǒu kàng 皋 门 有 伉。
They set up palace door	nǎi lì yìng mén 迺 立 应 门，
They'd never seen before.	yìng mén qiāng qiāng 应 门 将 将。
They reared an altar grand	nǎi lì zhǒng tǔ 迺 立 冢 土，
To spirits of the land.	róng chǒu yōu xíng 戎 醜 攸 行。

Autumn Trees and Distant Mountains by Zhao Yong
秋林远岫图　赵雍　元代（1206–1368）

Autumn Trees and Distant Mountains by Zhao Yong (1289-1360). Zhao, son of Zhao Mengfu, was a painter of high caliber in the Yuan Dynasty. In this picture the delicately painted trees and rocks show the artist's superb technique.

平水岸边几株杂树萧瑟地矗立在坡石上，芦苇草在微风中摇曳。山石、树木画法严谨，功力深厚，深得赵孟頫真传。

赵雍（1289–1360），元代画家，是赵孟頫之子，功力不逊色其父。

The angry foe not tame
Feared our Duke Tan Fu's name.
Oaks and thorns cleared away,
People might go their way.
The savage hordes in flight
Panted and ran out of sight.

sì bù tiǎn jué yùn
肆不殄厥愠，
yì bù yǔn jué wèn
亦不陨厥问。
zuò yù bèi yǐ
柞棫拔矣，
xíng dào duì yǐ
行道兑矣。
kūn yí tuì yǐ
混夷駾矣，
wéi qí huì yǐ
维其喙矣。

The lords no longer strove;
King Wen taught them to love.
E'en strangers became kind;
They followed him behind.
He let all people speak
And defended the weak.

yú ruì zhì jué chéng
虞芮质厥成，
wén wáng guì jué shēng
文王蹶厥生。
yú yuē yǒu shū fù
予曰有疏附，
yú yuē yǒu xiān hòu
予曰有先后，
yú yuē yǒu bēn zòu
予曰有奔奏，
yú yuē yǒu yù wǔ
予曰有御侮。

Playing the Zither Under Pine Trees by Zhu Derun

松间横琴图　朱德润　元代（1206—1368）

Playing the Zither Under Pine Trees by Zhu Derun (1294-1365) of the Yuan Dynasty. Zhu was proficient in calligraphy, poetry writing and landscape painting. Shown here is a fine landscape drawing with poetic ambience.

奇异的古松下一位高士横琴正坐，另一位高士手指哗哗流动的山泉，还有一位独坐无语，中间酒盏静置，似乎琴声和水声涌出了画外。

朱德润（1294—1365），元代画家，精诗文、书法，山水画尤精。

THE RISE OF ZHOU

O God is great!
He saw our State,
Surveyed our land,
Saw how people did stand.
Dissatisfied
With Yin-Shang's side,
Then He would fain
Find out again
Another State
He did not hate.
His eyes turned west;
Our State was blessed.

Tai cut the head
Off the trunk dead
And hewed with blows

huáng yǐ
皇矣

huáng yǐ shàng dì
皇矣上帝，
lín xià yǒu hè
临下有赫。
jiān guān sì fāng
监观四方，
qiú mín zhī mò
求民之莫。
wéi cǐ èr guó
维此二国，
qí zhèng bù huò
其政不获。
wéi bǐ sì guó
维彼四国，
yuán jiū yuán duó
爰究爰度。
shàng dì zhǐ zhī
上帝耆之，
zēng qí shì kuò
憎其式廓。
nǎi juàn xī gù
乃眷西顾，
cǐ wéi yǔ zhái
此维与宅。

zuò zhī bǐng zhī
作之屏之，
qí zī qí yì
其菑其翳；
xiū zhī píng zhī
修之平之，

Vines on a Cliff by Jiang Tingxi (1669-1732) of the Qing Dynasty. In the painting vines wind round a tall, straight Chinese toon. Limpid stream and verdant orchids lend an idyllic appeal to the scene. The painter's style is quite similar to that of his contemporary Yun Shouping.

藤花脆弱的枝蔓环环盈绕在秀挺的椿树上，清清的小溪从树下流过，兰花在岸边自由自在地绽放着……。

蒋廷锡（1669—1732），清代画家，擅画河塘野趣，气韵生动，有恽寿平的风格韵味。

Vines on a Cliff by Jiang Tingxi

藤花山崖图　蒋廷锡　清代（1616—1911）

The bushy rows.
The rotten trees
And mulberries
Were cleared away
Or put in array.
God made the road
For men's abode.
King Tai was made
Heaven's sure aide.

God visited Mount Qi
And thinned oak tree on tree.
Cypress and pine stood straight;
God founded the Zhou State.
He chose Tai as its head
And Ji when Tai was dead.
Ji loved his brothers dear;
His heart was full of cheer.

qí guàn qí lì
其灌其栵。
qǐ zhī pì zhī
启之辟之，
qí chēng qí jū
其柽其椐。
ráng zhī tì zhī
攘之剔之，
qí yǎn qí zhè
其檿其柘。
dì qiān míng dé
帝迁明德，
guàn yí zài lù
串夷载路。
tiān lì jué pèi
天立厥配，
shòu mìng jì gù
受命既固。

dì xǐng qí shān
帝省其山，
zuò yù sī bá
柞棫斯拔，
sōng bǎi sī duì
松柏斯兑。
dì zuò bāng zuò duì
帝作邦作对，
zì tài bó wáng jì
自大伯王季。
wéi cǐ wáng jì
维此王季，
yīn xīn zé yǒu
因心则友。
zé yǒu qí xiōng
则友其兄，

Lotus Flower by Xi Wang

洛甫仙裳图　奚冈　清代（1616—1911）

Lotus Flower by Xi Wang (1746-1803) of the Qing Dynasty. In light ink, the painter portrayed with both delicate and freehand brushwork lotus leaves and a flower just emerging from water. Xi from Anhui Province was good at flower and landscape drawing, and particularly proficient in seal cutting. He and three other seal-engravers Ding Jing, Huang Yi and Jiang Ren were called the Three Masters of Xiling as they all lived in Hangzhou, Zhejiang Province. Xiling refers to Hangzhou where the famous Xiling Bridge is located.

以淡墨、淡彩粗笔写荷叶水草，花朵全用没骨法，工写兼顾，更显示出荷花的高贵清雅。
奚冈(1746—1803)，清代画家，安徽人。擅画花卉、山水，更精于篆刻，与篆刻家丁敬、黄易、蒋仁并称为“西泠四家”。

When Ji was head of State,
He made its glory great.
The House of Zhou was blest
North to south, east to west.

zé dǔ qí qìng
则笃其庆，
zài xī zhī guāng
载锡之光。
shòu lù wú sàng
受禄无丧，
yǎn yǒu sì fāng
奄有四方。

God gave King Ji
The power to see
Clearly right from wrong
That he might rule for long.
With intelligence great
He could lead the whole State;
He ruled with wisdom high,
Thus obeyed far and nigh.
In his son King Wen's days
People still sang his praise.
For God's blessings would run
To his son and grandson.

wéi cǐ wáng jì
维此王季，
dì duó qí xīn
帝度其心，
mò qí dé yīn
貊其德音。
qí dé kè míng
其德克明，
kè míng kè lèi
克明克类，
kè zhǎng kè jūn
克长克君。
wàng cǐ dà bāng
王此大邦，
kè shùn kè bǐ
克顺克比。
bì yú wén wáng
比于文王，
qí dé mǐ huǐ
其德靡悔。
jì shòu dì zhǐ
既受帝祉，
yì yú sūn zǐ
施于孙子。

Plum Blossoms and Rocks by Wu Changshuo

梅石图　吴昌硕　民国（1912—1949）

Plum Blossoms and Rocks by Wu Changshuo (1844-1927). In this fan painting the artist drew plum blossoms and rocks with ease and verve. Wu, a modern-time painter, calligrapher and seal-engraver, was quite well-known to the public both in China and Japan.

小小的扇面上，用如此粗犷的笔墨，写出红梅与山石，真是胸中逸气的酣畅表达。

吴昌硕（1844—1927），近代书画家、篆刻家，绘画融篆刻、书法于一炉，以雄劲古朴的气势自创一格，在中国和日本影响极大。

To our King Wen God said,	dì wèi wén wáng 帝谓文王，
"Don't let the foe invade	wú rán pàn yuán 无然畔援，
Your holy land with might;	wú rán xīn xiàn 无然歆羡，
First occupy the height."	dàn xiān dēng yú àn 诞先登于岸。
The Mi tribe disobeyed,	mì rén bù gōng 密人不恭，
On our land made a raid,	gǎn jù dà bāng 敢距大邦，
Attacked Yuan and Gong State;	qīn ruǎn cú gōng 侵阮徂共。
King Wen's anger was great.	wáng hè sī nù 王赫斯怒，
He sent his troops in rows	yuán zhěng qí lǚ 爰整其旅，
To stop invading foes	yǐ àn cú lǚ 以按徂旅。
That the Zhou House might stand	yǐ dǔ yú zhōu hù 以笃于周祜，
And rule over the land.	yǐ duì yú tiān xià 以对于天下。
The capital gave order	yī qí zài jīng 依其在京，
To attack from Yuan border	qīn zì ruǎn jiāng 侵自阮疆，
And occupy the height.	zhì wǒ gāo gāng 陟我高冈。
Let no foe come with might	wú shǐ wǒ líng 无矢我陵，
Near our hill or our mountain	wǒ líng wǒ ē 我陵我阿；

Autumn View from a Garden by Wang Wu of the Qing Dynasty. The picture portrays a sleeping mynah on a plum branch, presenting an air of tranquility and harmony.

一只八哥熟睡在倒挂的白梅枝上，枝下水波荡漾。画面设色淡雅，八哥以工笔细描，梅枝造型舒展，气氛静谧而和谐。

Autumn View from a Garden by Wang Wu

老圃秋容图　王武　清代（1616–1911）

Nor to drink from our fountain
Nor our pools filled by rain.
King Wen surveyed the plain,
Settled and occupied
Hillside and riverside.
As great king he would stand
For people and the land.

To our King Wen God said,
"High virtue you've displayed.
You're ever lenient
To deal out punishment.
Making no effort on your part,
You follow me at heart."
To our King Wen God said,
"Consult allied brigade,
Attack with brethren strong,
Use scaling ladders long

wú yǐn wǒ quán
无饮我泉，
wǒ quán wǒ chí
我泉我池。
duó qí xiān yuán
度其鲜原，
jū qí zhī yáng
居岐之阳，
zài wèi zhī jiāng
在渭之将。
wàn bāng zhī fāng
万邦之方，
xià mín zhī wáng
下民之王。

dì wèi wén wáng
帝谓文王，
yú huái míng dé
予怀明德，
bù dà shēng yǐ sè
不大声以色，
bù cháng xià yǐ gé
不长夏以革；
bù shí bù zhī
不识不知，
shùn dì zhī zé
顺帝之则。
dì wèi wén wáng
帝谓文王，
xún ěr qiú fāng
询尔仇方，
tóng ěr xiōng dì
同尔兄弟；
yǐ ěr gōu yuán
以尔钩援，

A Double Blessing by Gao Qian

春王双喜图　高乾　清代（1616–1911）

A Double Blessing by Gao Qian of the Qing Dynasty. The painter drew a pair of magpies and blooming flowers with both delicate and freehand brushwork, implying fortune and happiness.

此幅画为兼工带写画法，芳花怒放，喜鹊成双，寓意身份高贵，喜事连连，福事双至之意。

And engines of assault
To punish Chong tribe's fault."

The engines of on-fall
Attacked the Chong State wall.
Many captives were ta'en
And left ears of the slain.
Sacrifice made afield,
We called the foe to yield.
The engines of on-fall
Destroyed the Chong State wall.
The foe filled with dismay,
Their forces swept away.
None dared insult Zhou State;
All obeyed our king great.

yǔ ěr lín chōng
与尔临冲，
yǐ fá chóng yōng
以伐崇墉。

lín chōng xián xián
临冲闲闲，
chóng yōng yán yán
崇墉言言。
zhí xùn lián lián
执讯连连，
yōu guó ān ān
攸馘安安。
shì lèi shì mà
是类是祃，
shì zhì shì fù
是致是附，
sì fāng yǐ wú wǔ
四方以无侮。
lín chōng fú fú
临冲茀茀，
chóng yōng yì yì
崇墉仡仡。
shì fá shì sì
是伐是肆，
shì jué shì hū
是绝是忽，
sì fāng yǐ wú fú
四方以无拂。

Flowers by Zhao Zhiqian

花卉图　赵之谦　清代（1616–1911）

Flowers by Zhao Zhiqian of the Qing Dynasty. During the florescence of peach trees in north China, they are usually in blossom before coming into leaf. In this sketch the red peach blossoms and the green leaves set each other off, a scene peculiarly seen in the south.

南方的桃花开放时，已长出叶子，花朵疏落，而北方的桃花开放时却是花朵“灼灼其华”，非常繁茂。本图轻松疏落的桃花恰与北方的景象形成对比。

HOU JI, THE LORD OF CORN

Who gave birth to the Lord of Corn?
By Lady Jiang Yuan he was born.
How gave she birth to her son nice?
She went afield for sacrifice.
Childless, she prayed for a son, so
She trod on the print of God's toe.
She stood there long and took a rest,
And she was magnified and blessed.
Then she conceived, then she gave birth,
It was the Lord of Corn on earth.

When her carrying time was done,
Like a lamb slipped down her first son.
Of labor she suffered no pain;

shēng mín
生民

jué chū shēng mín
厥初生民，
shí wéi jiāng yuán
时维姜嫄。
shēng mín rú hé
生民如何？
kè yīn kè sì
克禋克祀，
yǐ fú wú zǐ
以弗无子。
lǚ dì wǔ mǐn xīn
履帝武敏歆。
yōu jiè yōu zhǐ
攸介攸止。
zǎi zhèn zǎi sù
载震载夙，
zǎi shēng zǎi yù
载生载育，
shí wéi hòu jì
时维后稷。

dàn mí jué yuè
诞弥厥月，
xiān shēng rú dá
先生如达，
bù chè bù pì
不坼不副，

Landscape by Yuan Jiang

山水图　袁江　清代（1616—1911）

Landscape by Yuan Jiang of the Qing Dynasty. Characters in the painting walk in the snow. A bright moon hangs in the sky, illuminating a couple of withered trees. What a charming night scene!

枯树在风中摇动，白雪在初升月光的照耀下，显得格外洁净，主人踏雪归家，好象一股寒气直扑观者面颊。袁江（？—1746），江苏扬州人，清代画坛高手。

She was not hurt, nor did she strain.
How could his birth so wonderful be?
Was it against Heaven's decree?
Was God displeased with her sacrifice
To give a virgin a son nice?

wú zāi wú hài
无菑无害，
yǐ hè jué líng
以赫厥灵。
shàng dì bù níng
上帝不宁，
bù kāng yīn sì
不康禋祀，
jū rán shēng zǐ
居然生子。

The son abandoned in a lane
Was milked by the cow or sheep.
Abandoned in a wooded plain,
He's fed by men in forest deep.
Abandoned on the coldest ice,
He was warmed by birds with their wings.
When flew away those birds so nice,
The cry was heard of the nursling's.
He cried and wailed so long and loud
The road with his voice was o'erflowed.

dàn zhì zhī ài xiàng
诞寘之隘巷，
niú yáng féi zì zhī
牛羊腓字之；
dàn zhì zhī píng lín
诞寘之平林，
huì fá píng lín
会伐平林；
dàn zhì zhī hán bīng
诞寘之寒冰，
niǎo fù yì zhī
鸟覆翼之。
niǎo nǎi qù yǐ
鸟乃去矣，
hòu jì gū yǐ
后稷呱矣。
shí tán shí xū
实覃实訏，
jué shēng zài lù
厥声载路。

Autumnal Moonlight by Ma Hezhi

月色秋声图　马和之　南宋（1127—1279）

Autumnal Moonlight by Ma Hezhi of the Southern Song Dynasty. In the painting an old man sitting under a tree turns round to fix his eyes on the sparkling lake. The moonlight on the lake adds to the beauty of the scene.

曲曲的沙堤上，一长者悠然回望，侍者立其旁，这是一个秋日的傍晚，月光洒在白白的沙堤上，绿树在轻轻摇曳，画中的长者似乎要醉倒在这美丽的月光下……。

He was able to crawl aground
And then rose to his feet.
When he sought food around,
He learned to plant large beans and wheat.
The beans he planted grew tall;
His millet grew in rows;
His gourds teemed large and small;
His hemp grew thick and close.

The Lord of Corn knew well the way
To help the growing of the grain.
He cleared the grasses rank away
And sowed with yellow seed the plain.
The new buds began to appear;
They sprang up, grew under the feet.
They flowered and came into ear;
They drooped down, each grain complere.

dàn shí pú fú
诞实匍匐，
kè qí kè nì
克岐克嶷，
yǐ jiù kǒu shí
以就口食。
yì zhī rěn shū
蓺之荏菽，
rěn shū pèi pèi
荏菽旆旆。
hé yì suì suì
禾役穟穟，
má mài měng měng
麻麦幪幪，
guā dié běng běng
瓜瓞唪唪。

dàn hòu jì zhī sè
诞后稷之穑，
yǒu xiàng zhī dào
有相之道，
fú jué fēng cǎo
茀厥丰草，
zhòng zhī huáng mào
种之黄茂。
shí fāng shí bāo
实方实苞，
shí zhǒng shí yòu
实种实褎，
shí fā shí xiù
实发实秀，
shí jiān shí hǎo
实坚实好，

Almond Blossoms and Mandarin Ducks, author unknown. The almond blossoms painted on an enlarged scale look charming and lovely. Judging from the meticulous and precise style, it's a drawing made in the early years of the Yuan Dynasty. It has a flavor of the imperial-court decorative painting, but different from the latter's over-punctiliousness in method.

本幅从风格上看应是元代早期绘画，画风工细严谨，鸳鸯造型写真自然，杏花用夸张的手法加大了比例，显得天真可爱。画风有院体风格，但又松紧适中，区别于院体绘画过于刻板的习气。

Almond Blossoms and Mandarin Ducks

杏花鸳鸯图　无款　元代（1206—1368）

They became so good and so strong,
Our Lord would live at Tai for long.

shí yǐng shí lì
实颖实栗。
jí yǒu tái jiā shì
即有邰家室。

Heaven gave them the lucky grains
Of double-kernelled millet black
And red and white ones on the plains,
Black millet reaped was piled in stack
Or carried back on shoulders bare.
Red and white millet growing nice
And reaped far and wide, here and there,
Was brought home for the sacrifice.

dàn jiàng jiā zhǒng
诞降嘉种:
wéi jù wéi pī
维秬维秠,
wéi mén wéi qǐ
维穈维芑。
gèng zhī jù pī
恒之秬秠,
shì huò shì mǔ
是获是亩;
gèng zhī mén qǐ
恒之穈芑,
shì rén shì fù
是任是负;
yǐ guī zhào sì
以归肇祀。

What is our sacrifice?
We hull and ladle rice,
We sift and tread the grain,
Swill and scour it again.
It's steamed and then distilled;

dàn wǒ sì rú hé
诞我祀如何?
huò chōng huò yóu
或舂或揄,
huò bǒ huò róu
或簸或蹂,
shì zhī sōu sōu
释之叟叟,
zhēng zhī fú fú
烝之浮浮。

Phoenixes (partial) by Wu Huan of the Qing Dynasty. Wu, alias Mingshan, came from Wuxian, Jiangsu Province. The dates of birth and death are unknown. He lived around the first half of the 18th century. In rich colors the painting depicts peony flowers and a pair of phoenixes with smooth, delicate strokes.

此图画牡丹花下一对凤凰，形象秀丽、高雅，羽毛齐整，色彩绚丽，集众禽之美，其线条圆劲流畅，透出一股清逸仙雅之气。吴焕，生卒年不详，字铭山，江苏吴县人，约活动于18世纪前半叶。

Phoenixes (partial) by Wu Huan

凤凰石（局部） 吴焕 清代（1616–1911）

We see the rites fulfilled.

We offer fat with southernwood

And a skinned ram as food.

Flesh roast or broiled with cheer

Brings good harvest next year.

zài móu zài wéi
载谋载惟，

qǔ xiāo jì zhī
取萧祭脂，

qǔ dī yǐ bá
取羝以軷，

zài fán zài liè
载燔载烈。

yǐ xīng sì suì
以兴嗣岁。

We load the stands with food,

The stands of earthernware or wood.

God smells its fragrance rise;

He's well pleased in the skies.

What smell is this, so nice?

It's Lord of Corn's sacrifice.

This is a winning way;

It's come down to this day.

áng chéng yú dòu
卬盛于豆，

yú dòu yú dēng
于豆于登。

qí xiāng shǐ shēng
其香始升，

shàng dì jū xīn
上帝居歆，

hú xiù dǎn shí
胡臭亶时？

hòu jì zhào sì
后稷肇祀，

shù wú zuì huǐ
庶无罪悔，

yǐ qì yú jīn
以迄于今。

Fruits of the Season by Zhao Zhiqian of the Qing Dynasty. The artist painted in rich colors trees overhung with fruits. Peaches on the left scroll symbolize longevity while pomegranates on the right imply fertility and fortune in Chinese tradition.

画中花果和树木，笔墨厚朴，设色浓艳，硕果累累。构图疏密对比，题识书法厚拙朴实。右幅石榴寓意“多子多福”，左幅蟠桃寓意“长寿”，象征兴旺长寿之意。

Fruits of the Season by Zhao Zhiqian

四时果实图　赵之谦　清代（1616—1911）

DUKE LIU

Duke Liu was blessed;
He took nor ease nor rest.
He divided the fields
And stored in barns the yields.
In bags and sacks he tied
Up grain and meat when dried.
He led people in rows,
With arrows and drawn bows.
With axes, shields and spears,
They marched on new frontiers.

Duke Liu would fain
Survey a fertile plain
For his people to stay.

gōng liú
公 刘

dǔ gōng liú
笃公刘，
fěi jū fěi kāng
匪居匪康。
nǎi yì nǎi jiāng
迺场迺疆，
nǎi jī nǎi cāng
迺积迺仓。
nǎi guǒ hóu liáng
迺裹餱粮，
yú tuó yú náng
于橐于囊。
sī jí yòng guāng
思辑用光。
gōng shǐ sī zhāng
弓矢斯张，
gān gē qī yáng
干戈戚扬，
yuán fāng qǐ xíng
爰方启行。

dǔ gōng liú
笃公刘，
yú xū sī yuán
于胥斯原。
jì shù jì fán
既庶既繁，

Bridge and Mountain Landscape by Sheng Mao
野桥山水图　盛懋　元代（1206—1368）

Bridge and Mountain Landscape by Sheng Mao of the Yuan Dynasty. The picture has mansions, trees and people walking across a bridge in the foreground. Distant mountains are vaguely visible in a sea of clouds. Influenced by his contemporary painter Zhao Mengfu, Sheng's painting has a style of elegance and refinement.

溪桥上行人匆匆过往，不远处的一座豪宅庭院好像就是要到达的目的地，远山重叠，近景苍翠的杂树疏落有致，曲曲的溪水消失在交错的坡岸间，作品用笔疏简圆劲，墨色浓淡相间，变化微妙。
盛懋，元代画家，画风受赵孟頫影响，中正而秀雅。

On that victorious day
No one would sigh nor rest.
He came up mountain-crest
And descended again.
We saw his girdle then
Adorned with gems and jade,
His precious sword displayed.

Duke Liu crossed the mountains
And saw a hundred fountains.
He surveyed the plain wide
By the southern hillside.
He found a new capital
Wide for his people all.
Some thought it good for the throng;
Others would not dwell there for long.
There was discussion free;

jì shùn nǎi xuān
既顺迺宣，
ér wú yǒng tàn
而无永叹。
zhì zé zài yǎn
陟则在巘，
fù jiàng zài yuán
复降在原。
hé yǐ zhōu zhī
何以舟之？
wéi yù jí yáo
维玉及瑶，
bǐ běng róng dāo
鞞琫容刀。

dǔ gōng liú
笃公刘，
shì bǐ bǎi quán
逝彼百泉，
zhān bǐ pǔ yuán
瞻彼溥原；
nǎi zhì nán gāng
迺陟南冈，
nǎi gòu yú jīng
乃觏于京。
jīng shī zhī yě
京师之野，
yú shí chǔ chù
于时处处，
yú shí lú lǚ
于时庐旅，
yú shí yán yán
于时言言，

Goshawk and Ancient Pine by Zhang Shunzi, Xue Jieweng

黄鹰古桧图　张舜咨、雪界翁　元代（1206—1368）

Goshawk and Ancient Pine by Zhang Shunzi and Xue Jieweng of the Yuan Dynasty. The eagle painted by Xue with fine, delicate strokes and the pine tree by Zhang in freehand brushwork form a delightful contrast. Zhang and Xue were both good at landscape and pine drawing.

张舜咨画松树以水墨写意而成，枝干苍劲，雪界翁画苍鹰，刻画精微工整细致，是宋代院体画。二者一工一写既不相同又相应成辉，两位作者就是在这样的合作中得到心灵的沟通。张舜咨、雪界翁二人都是元代的画家，擅画山水、松柏。

They talked in high glee.	yú shí yǔ yǔ 于时语语。
Duke Liu was blessed;	dǔ gōng liú 笃公刘，
At capital he took rest,	yú jīng sī yī 于京斯依。
Put stools on mats he spread	qiāng qiāng jǐ jǐ 跄跄济济，
For officers he led.	bǐ yán bǐ jī 俾筵俾几。
They leant on stools and sat	jì dēng nǎi yī 既登乃依，
On the ornamented mat.	nǎi zào qí cáo 乃造其曹。
A penned pig was killed;	zhí shǐ yú láo 执豕于牢，
Their gourds with wine were filled.	zhuó zhī yòng páo 酌之用匏。
They were well drunk and fed;	sì zhī yìn zhī 食之饮之，
All hailed him as State head.	jūn zhī zōng zhī 君之宗之。
Duke Liu would fain	dǔ gōng liú 笃公刘，
Measure the hill and plain	jì pǔ jì cháng 既溥既长，
Broad and long; he surveyed	jì yǐng nǎi gāng 既景乃冈，
Streams and springs, light and shade;	xiāng qí yīn yáng 相其阴阳，

Boating on a Misty Lake by Kang Di

云浦行舟图　唐棣　元代（1206—1368）

Boating on a Misty Lake by Kang Di (1296-1334) of the Yuan Dynasty. Three hermits who go boating on a lake are enjoying the fine scenery on a midautumn day. The vast expanses of water and sky give play to one's fancy. Kang's painting has been deeply influenced by the Song Dynasty painters.

平湖上的一只小船，缓缓地驶离岸边，天空中一排大雁悠悠地飞向南方，此时正是仲秋时节，船上的三位高士，静静地欣赏着这美丽的秋色……。本图用平远法构图，画面开阔舒朗，笔墨之外空白处更是耐人寻味。
唐棣（1296—1334），元代画家，画风师法宋人，深得宋人遗意。

His three armies were placed
By the hillside terraced;
He measured plains anew
And fixed the revenue.
Fields were tilled in the west;
The land of Bin was blessed.

guān qí liú quán
观其流泉。
qí jūn sān dān
其军三单，
duó qí xí yuán
度其隰原，
chè tián wéi liáng
彻田为粮。
duó qí xī yáng
度其夕阳，
bīn jū yǔn huāng
豳居允荒。

Duke Liu who wore the crown
At Bin had settled down.
He crossed the River Wei
To gather stones by day.
All boundaries defined,
People worked with one mind
On the Huang Riverside
Towards Guo River wide.
The people dense would stay
On the shore of the Ney.

dǔ gōng liú
笃公刘，
yú bīn sī guǎn
于豳斯馆。
shè wèi wéi luàn
涉渭为乱，
qǔ lì qǔ duàn
取厉取锻。
zhǐ jī nǎi lǐ
止基迺理，
yuán zhòng yuán yǒu
爰众爰有。
jiá qí huáng jiàn
夹其皇涧，
sù qí guō jiàn
溯其过涧。
zhǐ lǚ nǎi mì
止旅乃密，
ruì jū zhī jí
芮鞫之即。

Profusion of Flowers (partial) by Qian Weicheng

万寿同春图（局部） 钱维成 清代（1616—1911）

Profusion of Flowers (partial) by Qian Weicheng (1720-1772) of the Qing Dynasty. Qian, the Number One Scholar (*zhuangyuan*) who came out first in the highest imperial examination during the reign of Emperor Qianlong, was skilled in flower drawing with the theme of auspicious happiness. With delicate, meticulous brushwork, the picture depicts sprays of flowers vying for beauty in full bloom.

图绘数种花卉绽放同一画面，每种都以折枝的形式表现，虽各自独立，但却姿态顾盼呼应，气息连贯，花朵枝叶刻画细致入微，是一幅吉庆喜气的花卉图卷。

钱维成(1720—1772)，清代画家，乾隆时期的状元，擅画吉庆题材的花卉图。

THE RISE OF SHANG

The Sire of Shang was wise;
Good omens had appeared for long.
Seeing the deluge rise,
He helped Yu stem the current strong,
Extend the State's frontier
And domain far and wide.
He was son born from Swallow queer
And Princess of Rong, its bride.

He held successful sway
Over states large and small.
He followed his proper way
To inspect all and instruct all.
Xiang Tu, his martial grandson,

长发

chǎng fā
长发

jùn zhé wéi shāng
濬哲维商，
cháng fā qí xiáng
长发其祥。
hóng shuǐ máng máng
洪水芒芒，
yǔ fū xià tǔ fāng
禹敷下土方。
wài dà guó shì jiāng
外大国是疆，
fú yuán jì cháng
幅陨既长。
yǒu sōng fāng jiāng
有娀方将，
dì lì zǐ shēng shāng
帝立子生商。

xuán wáng huán bō
玄王桓拨，
shòu xiǎo guó shì dá
受小国是达，
shòu dà guó shì dá
受大国是达。
shuài lǚ bù yuè
率履不越，
suì shì jì fā
遂视既发。

Flowers by Yun Shouping

花卉图　恽寿平　清代（1616—1911）

Flowers by Yun Shouping of the Qing Dynasty. The picture depicts magnolia branches embellished with a few blooming flowers and swelling buds. Branches and leaves are drawn in colors directly without first making sketches, a typical style of the painter.

柔柔的玉兰花，茸茸的花蕾，再加上没骨法写出的枝干穿插，是恽式花卉的典型风格。本幅款题“朱姿、粉黛、铁骨、金心”，八个字写出了作者所画花卉的全部含义。

Ruled over land and sea he had
won.

xiàng tǔ liè liè
相土烈烈，
hǎi wài yǒu jié
海外有截。

Heaven's favor divine
Lasted down to the Martial King.
Toward his lords benign,
In praise of God he'd often sing.
His virtue grows day by day ;
It is God he reveres.
God orders him to hold sway
And be model to the nine spheres.

dì mìng bù wéi
帝命不违，
zhì yú tāng qí
至于汤齐。
tāng jiàng bù chí
汤降不迟，
shèng jìng rì jī
圣敬日跻。
zhāo gé chí chí
昭假迟迟，
shàng dì shì zhī
上帝是祗，
dì mìng shì yú jiǔ wéi
帝命式于九围。

He received ensigns large and small
From subordinate princes far and
nigh.
He received blessings from gods all
For which he did nor seek not vie.
To lords he was nor hard nor soft;

shòu xiǎo qiú dà qiú
受小球大球，
wéi xià guó zhuì liú
为下国缀旒。
hè tiān zhī xiū
何天之休，
bù jìng bù qiú
不竞不絿，
bù gāng bù róu
不刚不柔，

Peach Blossoms and Fishing Boat by Wang Hui

桃花鱼艇图　王翚　清代（1616—1911）

Peach Blossoms and Fishing Boat by Wang Hui (1632-1717). Wang, alias Shigu, came from Changshu, Jiangsu Province. An outstanding landscape painter of a painting family, he made a big name in the early years of the Qing Dynasty. His painting won a commendation from Emperor Kangxi. The picture depicts an enchanting scene of spring in south China. Green hills and blue waters enveloped in mist and clouds are as gorgeous as fairyland.

青山翠树被层层的云雾盈绕得如仙境一般，独蓬的一只小艇从远远的桃花丛中驶出来，一幅江南春日的美景跃然纸上。图中山石、云烟、树木描绘得一丝不苟，功力非凡。

王翚，字石谷，清代画家，出身于绘画世家，曾得到康熙皇帝的赞赏，名声浩大。

His royal rule was gentle oft.
He received favors from aloft.

He received tributes large and small
From princes subordinate.
He received favors from gods all;
He showed his valor great.
Unshaken, he was fortified,
Unscared, unterrified.
All blessings came to his side.

His banners flying higher,
His battle-ax in his fist,
The Martial King came like fire
Whom no foe could resist.
Xie Jie was like the roots
Which could no longer grow
When he lost his three shoots,

fū zhèng yōu yōu
敷政优优，
bǎi lù shì qiú
百禄是遒。

shòu xiǎo gōng dà gōng
受小共大共，
wéi xià guó jùn páng
为下国骏厖。
hè tiān zhī chǒng
何天之龙，
fū zòu qí yǒng
敷奏其勇。
bù zhèn bù dòng
不震不动，
bù nǎn bù sǒng
不戁不竦，
bǎi lù shì zǒng
百禄是总。

wǔ wáng zài pèi
武王载旆，
yǒu qián bǐng yuè
有虔秉钺。
rú huǒ liè liè
如火烈烈，
zé mò wǒ gǎn è
则莫我敢曷。
bāo yǒu sān niè
苞有三蘖，
mò suì mò dá
莫遂莫达，

Bird on Budded Branch by Gao Qipei

花鸟图　高其佩　清代（1616—1911）

Bird on Budded Branch by Gao Qipei (1660-1734) of the Qing Dynasty. Gao practiced painting since childhood. After middle age he tried to paint with fingers in place of a brush, thus originating the peculiar finger painting. In this picture he drew with fingers the frightened bird and swelling buds on the branch, bringing about a marvelous effect.

独枝上的一只雀鸟正视读者，两眼齐瞪，象是惊恐欲飞的样子。如此生动的画面是作者用手指画出来的，枝干上的花蕾有明显的手指印，枝干则是手指甲的巧妙运用而达成的奇妙效果。

高其佩（1660—1734），清代画家，幼年始学画，中年后改用手指作画，形神兼备，是指头画派的创始人。

Wei, Gu, Kun Wu, Tang's former

foe.

The Martial King destroyed the brutes

And he ruled high and low.

In times when ruled King Tang,

There was prosperity for Shang.

Heaven favored his son

With Premier A Heng to run

The government and state

At left and right of the prince great.

jiǔ yǒu yǒu jié
九有有截，

wéi gù jì fá
韦顾既伐，

kūn wú xià jié
昆吾夏桀。

xī zài zhōng yè
昔在中叶，

yǒu zhèn qiě yè
有震且业。

yǔn yě tiān zǐ
允也天子，

jiàng yú qīng shì
降予卿士。

shí wéi ē héng
实维阿衡，

shí zuǒ yòu shāng wáng
实左右商王。

Goshawk, Chinese Parasol and Bamboo, without author's signature, drawn during the Yuan Dynasty. The artist drew the goshawk very meticulously while portraying the Chinese parasol tree and bamboos with freehand brushwork. As demonstrated by this picture, typically Yuan Dynasty painters inherited the realistic style from their Song Dynasty predecessors but broke with their formalist conceptions.

元代的绘画继承宋人写实、博大的精神，而把宋人过于严谨而略显刻板的习气大大突破。本幅花鸟画除苍鹰用极工细之笔外，梧桐树和修竹全用小写意之笔为之而构图又四平八稳，是典型的元人风格。

Goshawk, Chinese Parasol and Bamboo

苍鹰梧竹图　无款　元代（1206—1368）

图书在版编目(CIP)数据

精选诗经与诗意画／五洲传播出版社编；许渊冲译．
—北京：五洲传播出版社 2006.1
ISBN 7-5085-0887-4

Ⅰ．诗... Ⅱ．①五... ②许...
Ⅲ．古体诗－中国－春秋时代－汉、英
Ⅳ．I222.2

中国版本图书馆 CIP 数据核字(2005)第 151499 号

诗文翻译：许渊冲
辅文翻译：邵 达
图片编辑：蔡 程 任正炜

精选诗经与诗意画

出版发行：五洲传播出版社

策划编辑：荆孝敏 责任编辑：王 莉／荆孝敏
装帧设计：任正炜／屈银菊／谢 倩

社址：北京市海淀区北小马厂 6 号 邮政编码：100038
发行电话：010-58891281 传真：58891281
网址：www.cicc.org.cn

制版单位：北京紫航文化艺术有限公司
印刷：北京市华审彩色印刷厂
开本：720 × 980 1/16 印张：12.75

2006 年 2 月第 1 版，第 1 次印刷 印数：1-5000
ISBN 7-5085-0887-4/I・84 定价：78.00 元